Praise for *Millionaire Milestones*

"As the pioneer of the modern day FIRE movement, Dogen brings a fresh take on wealth-building strategies. Packed with practical advice on investing, entrepreneurship, and financial planning, this book empowers readers to surpass their financial goals and live the life they deserve."

—Jamie Fiore Higgins, author of *Bully Market* and former managing director at Goldman Sachs

"Building durable wealth has never been simple or easy. The problem is compounded by the constantly changing financial landscape. What worked yesterday no longer works today. What works today may not be appropriate tomorrow. Fortunately, Sam Dogen's *Millionaire Milestones* is an easy-to-read, clear-thinking guide to achieving that seven-figure nirvana. Sam never belabors the obvious nor trods the beaten path. His recommendations are always profoundly insightful, innovative, and fresh. And they are confirmed by his own personal success! If you haven't been able to achieve the wealth you dream of, I recommend Sam's book. It will kick-start you to a more financially rewarding life."

—Bill Bengen, financial advisor and creator of the 4% Rule

"Sam Dogen is one of the most original thinkers in personal finance. What sets Sam apart is extremely actionable insights, helpful benchmarks, and doing it all while prioritizing his family!"

—Noah Kagan, CEO of AppSumo and *New York Times* bestselling author of *Million Dollar Weekend*

"*Millionaire Milestones* is the ultimate playbook for anyone ready to take control of their financial future. With clear, actionable strategies for investing, entrepreneurship, and wealth building, Sam inspires you to think bigger and achieve more. This book isn't just about money. It's about creating freedom to live life on your terms."

—Humphrey Yang, personal finance YouTube influencer

"With surgical precision and refreshing candor, Sam Dogen dismantles the mythology surrounding wealth creation and replaces it with something far more valuable: a realistic road map to financial independence. Drawing from his own journey from Wall Street grinder to self-made millionaire, Dogen doesn't just tell you to save and invest—he shows you exactly how to think about money, deploy capital strategically, and avoid the psychological traps that derail even the smartest investors. The result is a masterwork of practical wisdom that transforms the complex into the actionable. For anyone serious about building lasting wealth while maintaining their soul, this book isn't just useful—it's essential."

— Jimmy Soni, bestselling author of *The Founders*

"I grew up poor and in public housing, with no one to teach me about money and no good role models. Learning about money always intimidated me, but *Millionaire Milestones* is the first book I've read that makes everything make sense in an approachable way. Sam not only provides both the tactics and the strategies to help you make the most of your money but there's a healthy dose of solid life advice to help you earn and save more. Highly recommended!"

—Ed Latimore, former heavyweight boxer and author
of *Hard Lessons from the Hurt Business*

"*Millionaire Milestones* is an indispensable guide to building wealth at any stage of life. What I appreciated most about this book is that it doesn't treat money as an end in and of itself, but rather as a means to a life well lived. Dogen breaks down how to live a rich life in a way that's accessible to everyone."

—Simone Stolzoff, author of *The Good Enough Job*

"Sam Dogen achieved millionaire status by age twenty-eight, and now he's sharing the blueprint. In *Millionaire Milestones*, Dogen revitalizes Napoleon Hill's timeless principles with seven clear, actionable steps. From uncovering your 'why' to sharpening your focus and taking bold action, this book lays out everything you need to build the wealth and life you deserve."

—Joe Saul-Sehy, creator and cohost of *Stacking Benjamins*

"*Millionaire Milestones* is going to change the way you think about money. Sam gives you a clear, step-by-step strategy to hit your seven-figure goals without having to sacrifice your life in the process. An essential addition to every enterprising person's bookshelf."

—David McKnight, author of *The Power of Zero*

MILLIONAIRE MILESTONES

MILLIONAIRE MILESTONES

Simple Steps to Seven Figures

SAM DOGEN

PORTFOLIO | PENGUIN

PORTFOLIO / PENGUIN

An imprint of Penguin Random House LLC
1745 Broadway, New York, NY 10019
penguinrandomhouse.com

Most Portfolio books are available at a discount when purchased in quantity for sales promotions or corporate use. Special editions, which include personalized covers, excerpts, and corporate imprints, can be created when purchased in large quantities. For more information, please call (212) 572-2232 or email specialmarkets@penguinrandomhouse.com. Your local bookstore can also assist with discounted bulk purchases using the Penguin Random House corporate Business-to-Business program. For assistance in locating a participating retailer, email B2B@penguinrandomhouse.com.

Interior art design by Colleen Kong-Savage.

BOOK DESIGN BY TANYA MAIBORODA

Library of Congress Cataloging-in-Publication Data

Names: Dogen, Sam, author.
Title: Millionaire milestones : simple steps to seven figures / Sam Dogen.
Description: New York : Portfolio/Penguin, [2025] | Includes bibliographical references.
Identifiers: LCCN 2024043395 (print) | LCCN 2024043396 (ebook) |
ISBN 9780593714706 (hardcover) | ISBN 9780593714713 (ebook)
Subjects: LCSH: Finance, Personal. | Investments. | Millionaires.
Classification: LCC HG179 .D58 2025 (print) | LCC HG179 (ebook) |
DDC 332.024—dc23/eng/20250129
LC record available at https://lccn.loc.gov/2024043395
LC ebook record available at https://lccn.loc.gov/2024043396

Printed in the United States of America
1st Printing

The authorized representative in the EU for product safety and compliance is Penguin Random House Ireland, Morrison Chambers, 32 Nassau Street, Dublin D02 YH68, Ireland, https://eu-contact.penguin.ie.

To Justy, whose joy knows no bounds,
and Keiah, whose heart swirls with kindness

Contents

A First Glimpse at Fortune

"TAKE YOUR DOG COLLAR OFF," yelled Mason, my manager. He was a Londoner in New York City, and we secretly referred to him as Evil English. He looked like Mr. Burns from *The Simpsons*, and he was as stingy with his compliments as he was generous with his tongue-lashings.

I had arrived to work at 5:30 a.m. wearing a puka shell necklace. Goldman Sachs had recently instituted a business casual dress code to help it compete against the growing tech firms who hired from the same talent pool. I figured, why not test out the new policy? My island-born parents—my dad from Oahu, my mom from Taiwan—had infused in me an easygoing vibe. That disappeared soon after I started working on the trading floor at what, at the time, was the most revered investment bank in the world.

"Right away, Mason!"

I sheepishly took off the necklace and shoved it in my drawer, red from embarrassment for being called out in front of my peers. I already felt like I didn't fit in. Graduates from the College of William & Mary, the public university in Virginia I had attended, weren't common hires at Goldman Sachs. Wealthy Ivy League graduates with rich and powerful parents were the norm. Among my entering analyst classmates' parents were a former prime minister of Canada, a high-ranking Chinese government official, and Goldman Sachs private clients with at least $25 million in investable assets—to name just a few. Hiring the progeny of the world's rich and powerful was good for business. Take care of someone's children, and they will take care of you. After all, children are parents' most valuable assets.

Then there was me, a guy who went to a public high school, a public college, and had no idea which utensil to use for each type of food during our many analyst dinners. Let's face it, my family had little to offer except for hard work and diversity. Whereas my fellow first-year analysts were used to attending fancy soirées and dressing to the nines, I wore whatever was on sale in my size at the local Century 21.

"Buy a black suit that fits and make sure it fits for the next ten years," advised one vice president during the analyst training period. It was his way of saying, *stay in shape if you know what's good for you.*

At Goldman, the name of the game was assimilation. If you wanted to get ahead, you needed to act like you belonged. If your boss liked Premier League football, so did you. If your VP with two children never left before eight p.m., there was no way in hell you could leave any earlier. In other words: Look the part. Live the part.

To survive, I very quickly stripped away my sense of self. After going through fifty-five interviews over seven rounds, I felt like I had won the lottery. I had a job at a premier investment bank in New York City. I wasn't about to screw things up!

And I didn't. More than that, I was successful at my job. But after the Twin Towers came down on September 11, 2001, I started questioning the purpose of working in finance. Was my entire career really going to be just about helping institutional investors make more money, or could I eventually find another occupation that provided more meaning and fulfillment?

I calculated that I had, at most, eighteen years of the Wall Street grind left in me before I would burn out. By then, I would have seen all the ugliness behind the façade and known I needed to plan my escape. Getting out at the age of forty sounded like a nice, round goal. I could spend the first half of my life bludgeoning my soul for money and spend the second half healing.

The problem was, I didn't have a clear road map to guide me to an escape hatch, or a money coach to help me navigate my way forward. What I did have was a primal fear of drowning in misery and dying young from exhaustion. That was more than enough motivation for me to exercise my wits and draw my own darn map.

Along the way, I made plenty of mistakes and suboptimal decisions, but I did what I could to learn from them, and I kept at it. I cut expenses everywhere I could—from sharing a tiny studio apartment with my buddy from high school to taking home leftovers from the office cafeteria to save on groceries. Most importantly, I went beyond budgeting and focused on income generation and investing. I started maxing out my 401(k). I boldly asked for raises and promotions. I threw whatever money I could into the stock market. Idle cash made me squeamish. I had a constant itch to put as much of my money *to work* as possible. Sometimes my bets were totally wrong, and I lost hard-earned money—oh, how it hurt—but I never gave up. I kept at it. As my income and investment knowledge grew, so too did my curiosity and thirst for more.

I had momentum and, with that—hope.

Reaching the Millionaire Milestone

I became a millionaire by the age of twenty-eight. The truth is there was no one thing that put me over the line. I just did the best I could and went with what I thought made the most sense.

Each goal I set, and ultimately reached, was a landmark on my map to freedom and financial security. Over time, those markers formed a path that led me to more wealth than I ever thought possible. The route I took wasn't a straight line—there were plenty of wrong turns and dead ends—but it eventually got me to better and greater things. For this reason, I named those landmarks "millionaire milestones."

I like the term milestone because it reminds me of the time I've spent teaching and encouraging my children. Each time we unlock a new achievement, it is a moment of triumph. As with parenting, some financial milestones are obvious the moment they happen, while others only become clear in hindsight. Again, I was never handed a road map or a list of milestones to achieve, but, looking back, I can now see each of them clear as day. I've compiled all the best millionaire milestones into this book to provide you with the map I never had. I want to save you from the mistakes I made so you can focus on what really works.

Although my life after Wall Street has been dramatically different, and more satisfying, frugality and diligent saving have remained inherent to my core. Meeting and beating financial milestones remain part of my daily life. This is why, by age forty, I was able to generate six figures a year in passive income for both my wife and me to remain free—now and forever.

Your Luck Just Increased

In my *Wall Street Journal* bestseller, *Buy This, Not That*, I discuss the importance of thinking in probabilities before making any decision. If you can get to a 70 percent probability that you are making a good decision, go for it. Just have the humility to know that same decision can be a bad or suboptimal choice about 30 percent of the time. Unless you experience catastrophe, you will learn from your mistakes and become a better decision-maker over time.

After you finish reading this book, I believe your probability of becoming a millionaire in your lifetime will far surpass 70 percent. I'd be shocked if you didn't accumulate your first million within twenty years of employing the presented guidelines, if not much sooner. Becoming a millionaire is no longer a mythical level of financial success only a lucky few will ever achieve. Rather, most people who are intentional with their finances will achieve millionaire status.

There are plenty of books to help you on your way. What sets me apart from other how-to-get-rich authors is that I walk the talk, writing from relevant, firsthand experience. I earned an undergraduate degree in economics and an MBA with a finance emphasis from UC Berkeley, worked in investment banking for thirteen years, bought my first property at age twenty-six and my second by age twenty-eight, left the traditional workforce at thirty-four, worked my way to multiple six figures in annual passive income by thirty-nine, started the personal finance site FinancialSamurai.com in 2009, and continue to share my thoughts about finance there regularly. I wasn't born rich, nor did I receive a trust fund or any cash inheritance. My parents raised me to be self-effacing and frugal. If you follow *Financial Samurai*, you know that I'm never too proud to admit when I'm wrong or discuss my mistakes.

Although I certainly appreciate the security and freedom

wealth provides, what has brought me greater, perpetual joy is helping others achieve their biggest hopes and dreams through financial independence. That's why I wrote this book.

The Road Ahead

Becoming a millionaire is not as hard as you may think—let me show you how.

We begin our journey with two chapters on the importance of perspective to get you in the right money mindset. From there, we will explore the three main phases on your journey to a million dollars: growth, lifestyle, and legacy. Along the way, I will teach you precise wealth-building strategies, show you how to eliminate financial anxiety, how to protect yourself from financial land mines and life's unexpected turns, and how to create both legacy and generational wealth for your family.

Becoming a millionaire is not easy, but, with enough time and direction, you can make it inevitable. Challenge yourself to complete each task in the end-of-chapter summaries and celebrate every time you check off each box.

As you embark on your journey, I want you to bear in mind these four principles:

1. **Adopt a prosperous mindset.** Believe in your ability to improve your finances and home in on super-specific purposes for growing your wealth.

2. **Get on the right side of growth.** Take your earning power momentum by the horns and invest for the long term.

3. **Live a life true to your values.** When you don't compromise your values, you not only feel richer, you become richer.

4. **Leave a meaningful legacy.** Get to the point where you can spend down your wealth with intention and significance.

Leapfrog 99.9 percent of the population when it comes to understanding money and building wealth by following the guidelines in this book. Customize them to your unique circumstances and goals and take control of your financial destiny.

You deserve to be rich, because you deserve to be free!

Now let's get started.

Perspective—Seize the Millionaire Mindset

MONEY. WE'RE OBSESSED WITH IT. HOW DO WE GET more of it?

In this section, I'll guide you through a thought exercise to unveil your true reasons for chasing that seven-figure dream. We'll delve into the realm of today's millionaires—exploring who they are, how they got there, and what sets them apart.

And here's the kicker: you're next in line. Yes, you. Millionaire status isn't just reserved for the lucky few. It's within your grasp, and I aim to provide essential groundwork and guide you through the journey, breaking it down into manageable milestones, step-by-step. Together, we'll pave the path toward financial success.

It's now time to learn exactly what it is about money that gets your heart racing. We're going to answer all the big whys and launch your wealth-building milestones into action.

Get excited—here we go!

Find Your Why

WE ALL WANT TO BE MILLIONAIRES, but why? Articulating your own unique answer will positively influence your wealth journey and help lay out a road map for success. Start by answering these main questions:

1. What's your motivation to save? In other words, what are the first three things you would do with a million dollars?

2. What purposes would a million dollars serve for you, and how would it change your life from what it is now?

Have you ever sat down and really thought about why you want to become a millionaire? For many people, the main goal is to secure their financial future for retirement. That purpose may not have the zing you're looking for, but trust me, after a lifetime of work, the last thing you want is to feel too financially insecure to actually retire.

Perhaps your reasons for getting rich are something else entirely. Maybe you are laser focused on the now, such as buying a house, paying for a loved one's surgery, affording steep tuition costs for two kids, or funding your own start-up. Whatever the reason, you need to have a clear purpose in mind.

Why a Clear Purpose Is a Fundamental Requisite to Wealth

You'd be surprised by how many people go through life aimlessly and fail to build wealth simply because they lack clarity and purpose. Wanting to get rich simply because adulting is expensive is not specific enough to get you to a million dollars. The general desire to afford more things and improve your lifestyle is understandable, but it's too vague. Over time, vagueness and a lack of concrete objectives tends to induce people to overspend, undercontribute to their savings and investment accounts, and drift significantly from their desired path.

A lack of clear purpose also makes it harder to motivate yourself to succeed. Just think about how many New Year's resolutions you failed to follow through on because your goal was too broad and lacked both direction and meaning. There's a big difference between *I want to buy a house* and *I want to save $300,000 for a down payment on a three-bedroom home over the next five years by saving 40 percent of my paycheck, investing in an S&P 500 ETF, and taking public transit instead of buying a car, because I want a place to raise a family.*

When it comes to growing wealth, target explicit, big-ticket expenses and detailed goals that span the coming years and decades. To achieve great success, hold yourself accountable over the long haul. The purposes you identify for building wealth will also influence how you choose to earn, keep, and spend your money. They can also guide you toward an ideal income level that balances your financial needs, happiness, sense of fulfillment, freedom, and time. Just like a racehorse in blinders, stop worrying so much about what everyone else is doing and get laser focused on your own path forward.

List Your Motivations for Greater Wealth

If you don't yet have a clear picture of what you want to do with a million dollars, spend the next five minutes writing down what you would love to do with it. Then, narrow down your list to the three most impactful applications. With the right mindset and specific purposes in hand, you will have the motivation and determination to make real, positive changes toward your pursuit of a million dollars.

Even if you already know why you want more money, chances are there are some other reasons you've overlooked. Here are some examples of various purposes greater wealth can serve in your life. Highlight your favorites and jot down any others you find particularly meaningful.

LIFESTYLE:

- To do what you want when you want
- To increase life expectancy (e.g., by comfortably affording better foods, health care, and safer transportation)
- To fly in comfort, travel the world, and experience new cultures
- To reveal your true self and be less fearful of judgment

FAMILY:

- To start a family (which may involve expensive fertility treatments and procedures)

- To spend more time with your children before they start school full time or leave home for good

- To give your children opportunities that weren't available to you

- To act as an insurance policy in case your children are unable to make a good living themselves

CAREER:

- To reduce your stress and work hours

- To have the freedom to say no to an unreasonable work request

- To tell your micromanager to jump in a lake

- To switch careers or work at a lower-paying job that provides more meaning and fulfillment

- To start your own entrepreneurial endeavors

- To retire early

VALUES:

- To spend more time helping people in need

- To speak up against injustice, bullies, bigots, and racists without fear of financial ruin

- To feel more secure in this brutally competitive world

- To give more to the most important charities

HEALTH:

- To get the best medical treatment possible for a disability or illness

- To pay for a private chef or dietician to improve your nutrition

- To not be afraid of the cost of going to the doctor or emergency room
- To hire personal trainers for any type of fitness goal
- To pay for a therapist

What comes to mind for you? Write down as many items as you can and make them specific.

_____

_____

_____

_____

_____

_____

Once you have a list of purposes in writing—yes, I want you to actually write your answers down or type them out—reorder your objectives, from greatest to least priority, and circle your top three. Now you have the precise motivation to save and invest for your future.

Having, Earning, and Spending a Million Dollars

Once you have a grasp on why you want to become a millionaire and the purposes the money will serve in your life, it's time to consider the differences between having a million dollars, earning a million dollars, and spending a million dollars. These differences will impact the timeline and strategies you use to acquire, maintain, and consume money.

Here's the good news: after a lifetime of saving and investing, if you achieve the milestones in this book, I'm confident you can get to a million-dollar net worth. And, depending on how your net worth is structured, having $1 million could generate $30,000 to $50,000 a year in a low-risk manner.

More difficult than acquiring that first million is earning seven figures a year. Earning a million dollars a year puts you in the top 0.1 percent of income earners in America. Getting to a top income requires longevity, hard work, and, well, a whole lot of luck!

Finally, spending a million dollars a year is actually the hardest to do of the three. To be able to spend a million dollars, you first need to accumulate a million dollars posttax. To spend a million dollars a year consistently, you need to have multiple millions of dollars (unless you want to end up broke). Anyone spending a million a year likely has a net worth of at least $50 million.

Be mindful of just how different one millionaire can be from the next. People achieve millionaire status in a multitude of ways and time frames. An awareness of the many roads to a million dollars can help prevent you from getting discouraged along the way. The route you take will be unique in duration and direction based on your own goals, choices, actions, and efficiencies (or lack thereof). There's no one right way to wealth and freedom. You get to choose your own path.

Keep in mind that your reasons for accumulating wealth will change as you age.

When I was in high school, I wanted money so I could buy a rich friend's 1990 Mustang 5.0 GT for $12,000. I imagined listening to the engine's sweet rumble while waiting outside my date's house before taking her to the movies. Alas, all I could afford was a bike.

At my first job at a major investment bank in New York City, I made a $40,000 base salary and could only afford a studio apartment with my high school buddy. The last thing I wanted was to rely on my parents for financial help. That would have been too embarrassing after four years of college and their financial support.

Now, as a father of two young children, I mainly want money to buy my wife and myself more time with our kids. It is estimated that by the time children turn nineteen, almost 90 percent of the time they will ever spend with their parents is already over. The image of our children graduating high school and finally leaving home is both joyful and sad. Time is our most precious commodity.

Having anticipated the ever-increasing scarcity of time as we age and the challenges of juggling work and raising children long before I became a father, I delayed having kids until I felt financially secure. I wanted to be able to care for my kids on my own schedule, not around the needs of a demanding employer. Unfortunately, I failed to consider that having children later means I'll be in their lives for less time. Now I'm doing my best to play catch-up.

As time passes, the main purposes you assign to your financial growth will also change. Pause, assess, pivot, and always keep evolving.

How Far Can a Million Get You?

Let's look at roughly how much some things can cost in your working years and in retirement to give you a better idea of what you can and can't do with $1 million.

$300,000	The average cost to raise a child until age eighteen
$200,000	Cost of two years at community college plus two more at a state school by the year 2042*
$651,000	The expected all-in cost of four years at a private university by the year 2042[†]
$315,000	Average health-care expenses for a sixty-five-year-old couple in retirement
$26,000	Average annual housing and transportation expenses for older retirees
$115,000	Average annual cost of a private nursing home room

* Assumes a two-year cost of $26,000 for tuition, fees, room, and board at a community college plus a two-year cost of $44,000 for in-state tuition, fees, room, and board at a public state school at a 6 percent annual compound growth rate for eighteen years.
[†] Assumes a four-year cost of $42,000 for tuition and fees plus $15,000 for room and board at a 6 percent annual compound growth rate for eighteen years.

Now that you have a sense of how far $1 million can take you, revisit your list of key purposes for earning wealth. Make revisions if you grossly underestimated how much you may need in retirement, or if your priorities shift. Your goals and motivations to save can help guide your decision-making as to what lifestyle changes will make becoming a millionaire more achievable more quickly.

Depending on your age and family situation, you may need at least $1 million just to make ends meet. The big three expenses are shelter, health care, and education. If you want to reduce your need for money, stay fit and don't have children. For the rest of us, who want kids and don't run ten miles after enjoying a cheeseburger, the cost of living will be much greater. Please choose your lifestyle accordingly.

The Ideal Income for Maximum Happiness

Nobody said becoming a millionaire is easy. Sacrifices must be made! For most of us, the sacrifice will be in the amount of time we spend on our careers. The harder and smarter you work each day, and cumulatively over time, the greater your chance of becoming a millionaire. But, at some point, we must all decide how much is enough. How much annual income is sufficient to achieve your goals? The answer is different for everyone, because everyone's desires and cost of living are different.

As someone whose salaries have ranged from $4 per hour working at McDonald's to much more as an entrepreneur, I believe happiness is more about family, friends, health, and purpose than about wealth. Once you earn enough to take care of your basic living expenses, what keeps you happy is better relationships, good health, and a strong purpose—not more money.

Think about the goals you wrote down. Go through your budget and calculate how much posttax income you need to cover everything comfortably. Then tack on 20 percent for saving and investing. This is your ideal income for maximum happiness.

For example, let's say for the past three years your family of four spends $8,000 a month on food, clothing, shelter, transportation, and miscellaneous items for a comfortable lifestyle. That's $96,000 a year. Multiply $96,000 by 1.2 to account for the 20 percent saving and investing, and you get $115,200. Thus, somewhere around $115,200 after tax would be your ideal, steady-state income level. Any additional income you could make over $115,200 would be unlikely to result in additional happiness in your life. Once you make about $100,000 per adult in the Midwest, or $250,000 per adult on the coast, both adjusted for inflation, there is no significant incremental increase in happiness as your income rises further.

For more perspective, in 2010, Nobel Prize winners Daniel Kahneman and Angus Deaton of Princeton University argued that $75,000 was the ideal income, above which happiness increased no further. If we adjust for inflation at a rate of 3 percent, that $75,000 equates to roughly $117,000 in 2025, $157,000 in 2035, and $182,000 in 2040. In 2023, Kahneman published a follow-up study, with coauthor Matthew Killingsworth of the University of Pennsylvania, claiming that happiness continues to rise up to $500,000 in annual income for most people. "The exception is people who are financially well-off but unhappy," Killingsworth explained. About 15–20 percent of people fall into this "unhappy minority." For them, additional income above $100,000 per year didn't have a major impact on their emotional well-being.

You may want to earn more than my suggested, inflation-adjusted $100,000 in the Midwest and $250,000 on the coast. If so, you should try to do so. Just be careful. The more active income you make, the more stressful your work will become. For example, when I was working in investment banking, the managing directors made the most money. They had base salaries of $400,000 and up and would regularly make $1 million in total compensation per year. They also had dozens of people to manage, were responsible for the profitability of various divisions in the firm, and were constantly stressed out. When downturns came, the MDs were often the first to be let go. CEOs of large companies might be making millions of dollars, but at what cost? With multiple direct reports, quarterly shareholder meetings, media scrutiny, nonstop business trips, and multiple fires to put out on a weekly basis, they have much less free time than the average person. Some hardly ever get to see their children grow up, which can result in their kids struggling with a lifetime of emotional damage. Studies even show that CEOs who experience unusual stress can lose roughly one to two years of life expectancy, which is the ultimate negative.

Now compare those CEOs with an average employee who gets to work forty hours a week or less, always has time to exercise, and reliably comes home in time to eat dinner with their family. Is a CEO's lifestyle really much better than that of the average person who has more control over their time and less stress? I'm not so sure. Time is more valuable than money, especially as you get older.

What may augment your happiness more than just making extra money is *how* you earn it. If you can increase the percentage of your total income derived from passive sources (e.g., stock dividends) versus active sources (e.g., your job), your happiness may improve further.

Whatever you're doing, whether it's a high-powered job, hustling as an individual contributor, or working for yourself, regularly revisit your purposes for wanting more money in the first place and consider how your choices are impacting your happiness.

Make the Money and Escape!

Earning a healthy salary is one part of the millionaire equation. Keeping and growing what's left of your salary after taxes and necessary expenses is the other part. Having specific net worth targets by age or number of years worked is key for your trek to a million. Otherwise, it is easy to blow your earnings on superfluous things that do not help you build wealth.

Here is a sample net worth target chart I put together for those looking for some wealth accumulation guidance. After six years of work experience, aim to accumulate a net worth equal to your average gross salary. After ten years of work experience, target a net worth equal to ten times your average gross salary. Ultimately, strive to accumulate at least ten times your average gross salary to start feeling free and twenty times your average gross salary, the ultimate stretch goal, to experience complete financial freedom.

Net Worth (NW) Targets by Age, Years Worked, and Income

Age	Years Worked	Multiple of Income = NW	NW Based on $50K	NW Based on $100K	NW Based on $150K	NW Based on $200K	NW Based on $300K	NW Based on $500K
22	0	0	–	–	–	–	–	–
25	3	0.5	$25,000	$50,000	$75,000	$100,000	$150,000	$250,000
28	6	1	$50,000	$100,000	$150,000	$200,000	$300,000	$500,000
30	8	2	$100,000	$200,000	$300,000	$400,000	$600,000	$1,000,000
32	10	3	$150,000	$300,000	$450,000	$600,000	$900,000	$1,500,000
35	13	5	$250,000	$500,000	$750,000	$1,000,000	$1,500,000	$2,500,000
40	18	10	$500,000	$1,000,000	$1,500,000	$2,000,000	$3,000,000	$5,000,000
45	23	13	$650,000	$1,300,000	$1,950,000	$2,600,000	$3,900,000	$6,500,000
50	28	15	$750,000	$1,500,000	$2,250,000	$3,000,000	$4,500,000	$7,500,000
55	33	18	$900,000	$1,800,000	$2,700,000	$3,600,000	$5,400,000	$9,000,000
60+	38	20	$1,000,000	$2,000,000	$3,000,000	$4,000,000	$6,000,000	$10,000,000

Source: FinancialSamurai.com

With a $50,000 income, you should target $500,000 to $1 million in net worth by the time you retire. But with a $500,000 average salary, aim for a $5 million to $10 million net worth. Either way, you'll accumulate a level of wealth that will likely take care of you for the rest of your life.

The great thing about basing your net worth targets on a multiple of income instead of on your expenses is that it imposes discipline. As your income grows, you are forced to stay disciplined in your saving and investing. If you use a multiple of your expenses to come up with a net worth target, you can cheat your way to that target by slashing expenses. You could claim to reach financial independence faster by limiting your diet to ramen noodles, but you'll be less likely to accumulate as large a nut as you could by targeting a multiple of your income, plus you'll have a harder time staying ahead of inflation over time. Once you reach your income-based targets, you can always dial back your lifestyle if you want.

There's a clear benefit to working your butt off to see how far you can go in your career. If you get to a six-figure income level, or even a seven-figure income level, aim for it to last for at least ten years and save 50 percent or more of your after-tax income. At a 50 percent posttax saving rate, every year you save equates to one year of freedom you buy on the back end. Let's say you make $100,000 posttax and save 50 percent. After one year, you would spend $50,000 and save $50,000. In this scenario, for every year you work and save 50 percent, you essentially buy yourself one year of financial freedom. A simple way to save 50 percent, if you have bimonthly paychecks, is to save and invest 100 percent of one entire paycheck each month.

Now, suppose you save 20 percent of your $100,000 posttax income. After a year, you spend $80,000 and save $20,000. This means for every year you work, you save 25 percent of one year's living expenses. With a 20 percent saving rate, it would take you four years of work to save enough for one year of living expenses. Finally, imagine you save 80 percent of your $100,000 posttax income. After a year, you would spend $20,000 and save $80,000. In this case, for every year you work, you save four years' worth of living expenses! Maintain this 80 percent saving rate for ten years, and you will have saved enough to cover forty years of living expenses, assuming your expenses remain constant.

As you progress further in your career, your ambitions will likely change. Just remember that high-income opportunities don't last forever. Maximize the opportunity while the window is still open, because you might never get to earn such a high income again. Eventually, you'll accumulate a large enough financial nest egg to do whatever your heart desires. Not a day goes by when I'm not thankful for working brutal hours in my twenties and early thirties to try to earn the maximum income for my occupation. Thirteen years of aggressive saving and investing were enough for me to break free from the corporate world. With the help of a severance package and $80,000 a year in passive investment income, I was able to take a leap of faith at age thirty-four. I knew I could always go back to work if my early retirement/writing lifestyle didn't work out.

If you decide to retire, it might feel weird giving up so much money at first. Golden handcuffs are incredibly tough to break. But I bet the value of your newfound freedom will far surpass any money you'll forsake. After I left corporate America in 2012, all my chronic pain (TMJ, lower back pain, sciatica, tennis elbow, golfer's elbow, etc.) went away. The health benefits of early retirement are priceless. And as you get older, you appreciate your freedom more because you are more aware of the dwindling time you have left.

If you've been contemplating whether to raise your saving rate by another 10 percent, do it. Once you're there, raise it by another 10 percent. You will quickly learn to live within your means. And if you've been debating working on a side hustle before or after work, the answer is yes. You never know what might become of it. Always remember that money is simply a tool for happiness. If you aren't happy, then you must make a change. Either save more, change careers, or take more calculated risks. You don't want to look back at life with regret.

The Downsides of Becoming a Millionaire

While there are lots of obvious benefits of becoming a millionaire, the process isn't without its downsides. Trying to become a millionaire will require you to get out of your comfort zone and work harder than you ever have before. There can be a lot of stress and misery on the road to a million dollars. You will likely have to work long hours, forsake valuable family time, experience tremendous stress, and take risks that will cost you money or time. During difficult times, step back and remind yourself of the reasons why you want to become a millionaire. As long as you never forget your why, you will be able to push through almost anything.

For me, I am afraid of losing too much money while my children are still young. If I do, I may have to sell our house, limit our educational activities, and perhaps ultimately go back to the kind of nine-to-five job I desperately escaped before having children. Now, the stakes are much higher with a family of four. Maybe when my children are independent adults, hopefully by their mid-twenties, I can pull a *Leaving Las Vegas* and bet it all on black. But not now.

Don't Confuse Million with Billion

With all that said, don't expect obtaining $1 million in wealth to transform your life into that of an ultrarich and famous billionaire. After all, one billion is one thousand times greater than one million. Plus, there are only about 2,781 billionaires in the world compared to more than 59.4 million millionaires. So, is it realistic to expect that someday you'll have enough money to buy a $65 million private jet or spend $165 million on your fifth mansion like Jeff Bezos? No. However, having $1 million today provides for a comfortable, middle-class to upper-middle-class retirement based on the passive income it can generate.

Just how much does the lifestyle of a billionaire really differ from that of a millionaire? Many millionaires live quite comfortably but may still have to work, budget expenses, and save for retirement. Billionaires, on the other hand, have so much excess wealth that they can freely live lavishly.

Billionaires, They're Just Like Us

A multimillionaire friend of mine spent a week vacationing on a billionaire's yacht with ten other guests. Upon his return, I asked my friend what the whole experience was like. What could billionaires do that the rest of us mere mortals could not?

He said, "Besides needing to sign nondisclosure agreements, having security detail follow us everywhere for protection, and eating any type of ice cream we wanted at any time, we mostly just hung out and enjoyed each other's company. Nobody knew who was coming on the trip, except for the hosts. It was an eclectic bunch of people from different backgrounds—entertainment, media, finance, e-commerce. We mainly shared stories and had a good time by simply hanging out."

Community is what matters most. You don't need to be a billionaire or even a millionaire to have a great time with a group of friends. According to the Harvard Study of Adult Development, the stronger our relationships, the more likely we are to live happy, satisfying, and healthy lives. We may not be able to host an island getaway on a private yacht with ten of the most sought-after people in the world, but we can throw a memorable dinner party anytime.

At the end of the day, if you want to beat the Joneses, you should compete on *freedom*. After all, there is always one more dollar to make but never another second. Your mission, if you choose to accept it, is to recognize how much money is enough and then proactively buy back as much time as you can with the money you have left.

To Contemplate:

- [ ] Decide if you want to achieve a million-dollar net worth or a million-dollar annual salary. The difference in net worth potential is huge, but there are risks and costs involved.

- [ ] The right mindset paired with clear purposes will give you the motivation and determination you need to achieve a million dollars through positive and constructive action steps.

- [ ] Your desires have a direct impact on your need for money. Concrete lifestyle changes can reduce or increase your need for money.

- [ ] Don't expect a billionaire lifestyle on a millionaire net worth. Instead, strive to be a time and health billionaire.

To Do:

- [ ] Identify your high-level endgame and motivations to become a millionaire.

- [ ] Next, write down ten or more specific purposes for achieving greater wealth in your life. Then circle your top three priorities.

- [ ] Use my chart *Net Worth Targets by Age, Years Worked, and Income* as a guide for wealth accumulation. This approach imposes more discipline by focusing on a multiple of your annual gross income, rather than just your expenses. Aim to accumulate ten times your average gross income to start feeling a sense of financial freedom.

- [ ] Calculate your ideal income for maximum happiness and to balance your financial needs. Go through your budget and calculate how much posttax income you need to cover everything comfortably. Then tack on 20 percent for saving and investing.

☐ Divide your current net worth by your average gross salary. Then compare that figure to the multiple of income in my net worth target chart for your age and years worked. Use it as a guide to adjust your earnings, saving, and investing goals to further boost your net worth.

Believe You Can Be a Millionaire Too

WHAT DO YOU ENVISION WHEN you hear the word *millionaire*? Perhaps you see a gray-haired retiree sipping coffee on a balcony overlooking a white, sandy beach. Or maybe you picture a famous actress or professional athlete instead. Whatever your ideal flavor of millionaire is, chances are you've unsuspectingly walked past many everyday millionaires whom you'd never suspect have a seven-figure net worth.

Millionaires are no longer ultrarare creatures that only come out in the pale moonlight. According to the annual UBS Global Wealth Report released in 2024, there were more than 59 million millionaires globally at the end of 2022. That equates to roughly 1 percent of all adults worldwide. The Federal Reserve's Survey of Consumer Finances released in 2023 reported that the average American household's net worth, adjusted for inflation, was $1.06 million—a 23 percent increase from 2019. Yes, that's right. The average American household is a millionaire, and some of those households consist of individuals! Of course, the median household net worth, a more representative figure, is only $192,000. The question is: Do you want to be median, average, or above average?

As a result of all that new wealth, an adult now needs roughly $1.1 million to belong to the global top 1 percent. But to be in the top 1 percent in America, an adult needs to have more than $11 million. Investment gains and inflation have really pushed the number of millionaires in the world to record highs. By 2030, a household will likely need a net worth of more than $15 million to be in the top 1 percent of households in America by wealth.

You may be wondering if this much growth in wealth is sustainable. UBS forecasts that the number of global millionaires isn't slowing but accelerating. By 2027, it estimates, there will be 86 million millionaires.

You've Got to Believe

I offer all these astonishing statistics because I want you to realize that you can be a millionaire too. From the unassuming millionaire next door who drives a beater car to the Vermont gas station janitor who amassed $8 million, people are quietly getting rich every day. You can too!

You need faith in yourself and your abilities and unwavering discipline to achieve greatness. Nobody else is going to put money in your bank account or save you from making poor financial decisions. Don't just sit around fidgeting and lamenting over what you don't have. Far too many people waste their entire lives feeling sorry for themselves. You need to believe you can get rich today so that you will maximize the time and energy you have left.

Now, with a striking 5.5 times difference between the average American household wealth ($1.06 million) and median household wealth ($193,000), ask yourself if you want to be median or average. Personally, I want to be as far *above* average as possible. I suspect you do too, given that you've picked up this book. Average people do not read personal finance books. Average people spend three hours a day watching TV and eating potato chips on the sofa. To live a special life, you must outperform, and you must not succumb to the herd mentality.

Ever since starting *Financial Samurai* in 2009, I've always recommended that readers aim to beat both the mean and median net worth figures in America. We only get one go at life, so we might as well make the most of it.

What Are the Chances of Becoming a Millionaire?

With an uneven playing field, not everyone's odds are the same. One's amount of sheer will and purpose are huge drivers in achieving a million dollars. The median income of your location also has a large impact. There are other equally important factors worth exploring. Let's take a look.

Becoming a Millionaire Is Easier If You Love Personal Finance

Over the last fifteen years, I've received countless emails from readers who busted through the $1 million net worth figure thanks to aggressive saving and investing. Many have also mentioned they wish they had discovered the personal finance world sooner. Better late than never, I say!

Financial Samurai readers have a higher likelihood of becoming millionaires than those who don't. Constant encouragement to save, invest, and focus on financial goals makes it almost inevitable that readers will build more wealth than the average person. They're engaged, learning, and sharing financial knowledge every day. Instead of being too afraid to invest their hard-earned cash, they take action by investing in risk assets that have historically appreciated over time. But what about everybody else? Let's look at the chances of becoming a millionaire in America based on data from the Federal Reserve Board.

Your Chances of Becoming a Millionaire by Race and Educational Attainment

Among middle-aged, college-educated Americans, people of Asian descent (who make up about 7 percent of the US population) have the highest probability of becoming a millionaire, at 22.3 percent. This is followed by a 21.5 percent chance for people who identify as white (58.9 percent of the population). However, Hispanic and Black Americans (19.1 percent and 13.6 percent of the population, respectively) have less than a 7 percent chance.

Data also shows that, across all races, the more education you receive, the higher your chances of becoming a millionaire. This makes sense, since high-paying jobs (e.g., lawyer, doctor, executive manager, engineer, and scientist) often require higher levels of education. However, thanks to free online learning and shorter specialty school programs, a college degree is slowly becoming devalued.

But what explains this huge difference between races? The first part of the answer is simple math. Compound interest is often referred to as the eighth wonder of the world. If you understand it, you can earn it. If you don't, you may wind up paying it. If your ancestors were able to earn more money, own more land, and invest in more assets for a longer period, of course they got wealthier than those who couldn't.

The second part of the answer is that people tend to take care of those who are most like themselves. If you are part of the majority, then you will have more opportunities to get ahead. Once you have money and power, there is a tendency to keep the wealth circulating among your own.

When I was working in the Asian equities department, the head, who was based in Hong Kong, was a white chap from England. To nobody's surprise, he appointed white, English heads at the offices in London and New York. When he left the firm, however, a Korean guy became the new boss. The English heads in London and New York then got laid off, and in came two Korean hires to take their places. Coincidence? Of course not.

I don't think most people are intentionally biased. I've just continually observed that people tend to befriend and support people with similar backgrounds. Just look around your own social group and workplace. I bet if you got a new boss from Tasmania, suddenly you would start to see a lot more Tasmanian associates. If your new boss is a woman, you'll likely get more female colleagues. If a company really wants to recruit a diverse group of employees, there needs to be diverse representation. Nobody wants to feel like the odd person out.

The main takeaway from these data points is to do ample research when looking for work. Be deliberate in your job selection. We can't change our racial makeup, but we can choose to join companies where we feel supported. Secondly, be intentional with your educational attainment. Learning shouldn't stop after college. Invest in your future by getting as highly educated as possible throughout your life. Deeper knowledge will increase your chances of greater wealth.

Your Chances of Being a Millionaire by Age

The earlier you start investing, the greater your chances of eventually becoming a millionaire. This is obvious thanks to compound returns. Just look at Warren Buffett. He started investing at age eleven in 1942. By his early thirties, he had become a millionaire, which, adjusted for inflation, was a net worth equivalent to more than $10 million in today's dollars.

Even as impressive as that is, most of Buffett's wealth came after his fiftieth birthday. He reached billionaire status at age fifty-six, $16.5 billion by age sixty-six, $35.7 billion by age seventy-two, $67 billion by age eighty-four, and roughly $136 billion by age ninety-three. And he's already given away more than $60 billion. Quite a feat.

Studies show that everybody's chances of becoming a millionaire improve up until the age of sixty-one, regardless of race. Use that time wisely to optimize as many financial decisions as possible.

You Are the Inevitable Millionaire

Check out the stats, but don't sweat the percentages. Here's the deal: if you're into personal finance, prioritize your cash flow, invest diligently, chase the goals you have laid out, and you'll have about a 75 percent shot at joining the millionaire's club. It's all about that mindset—stay positive, soak up knowledge, and watch your wealth stack up. You've got this. Becoming a millionaire? Totally doable.

THE *FINANCIAL SAMURAI* WAY

To Contemplate:

☐ Believe in your abilities, no matter what. An unwavering, confident, and positive money mindset is your secret weapon. If you don't believe in yourself, nobody else will.

To Do:

☐ Memorize these facts: The number of millionaires in the world is forecasted to grow by 8 percent a year for years to come. By 2027, it's estimated there will be eighty-six million millionaires.

☐ Now tell your best friend those facts you just memorized plus this statistic: There are more than twenty-four million millionaires in the US alone. That's 39 percent of the world's millionaires.

☐ Next, hold yourself accountable by telling someone you're close to that you've just made a pact to become a millionaire, and challenge them to do the same.

☐ Go grab a sticky note, notecard, or whiteboard, write the phrase "I can be a millionaire too!" on it, and put it somewhere you'll see it every day. Send me a copy of your pic at sales@financialsamurai.com for a chance to be included in my newsletter or on my blog.

Growth—Millionaire Fundamentals

THANKS TO INFLATION, IF YOUR WEALTH ISN'T GROW-ing, you're not just running in place, you're actually falling behind. Fortunately, the milestones in this book will not only help you beat inflation, they will likely help you achieve more wealth than you ever thought possible.

Too much financial literature is focused on budget tightening as the way to build wealth. But you can only save so much. Since your sights are set on reaching a million dollars, growth is what needs to be at the core of every financial decision you make as you navigate from one milestone to the next.

In this section, we'll cover the exponential potential of momentum, why $250,000 is a magical number, and why you should push through some aches and pains until you reach a 30 percent or greater saving rate. Plus, I'll explain why it's in your best interest to prioritize building your net worth more than your income from your job. We'll also discuss my favorite asset class for building wealth: real estate. It's not only my bread-and-butter area of expertise, it's also an exceptional path to greater wealth creation for the average person. Phase I will wrap up with a look at how the superrich are so heavily invested in business interests and entrepreneurship, and why it's beneficial for you to do the same.

Now let's get growing.

Harness the Power of Momentum

NEWTON'S FIRST LAW OF MOTION, also known as the law of inertia, states that an object at rest stays at rest, and an object in motion stays in motion unless acted upon by an unbalanced force. This principle is key to thinking about how you'll get your first million: the same saving and investing patterns that get you to one, smaller goal will carry you to your ultimate, larger goal.

First, start saving toward $10,000. This smaller goal will take the pressure off and allow you to build your saving and investing habits. That's the hard part. Once you have your routine set, the goal of earning your first million will seem less daunting. After $10,000, set your sights on accumulating $50,000, then $100,000, and then $250,000. The key to building great wealth is to save and invest consistently for as long as possible. Compound returns on your investments, which should increase each year, do the work for you.

Reasons Why Momentum Matters

Why did I ask you to set $250,000 as your goal, when it's only 25 percent of the way to $1 million? It is enough money for you to feel the meaningful results of all your hard work. And this feeling of reward, knowing that you can find success, will motivate you to keep on going until you reach $1 million. Otherwise, you'll give up long before you give yourself a real shot at great wealth.

Here's a great example. Eleven years of maxing out your 401(k) can get you to $250,000 based on contributions alone, and the IRS increases the maximum 401(k) contribution over time, which will accelerate your approach to $250,000 year by year. The best news? This doesn't include other helpful factors, like employer matching, profit sharing, or investment returns. Automating your 401(k) contributions and maximizing a company match, if you have access to one, will further accelerate your monetary growth through compounding. If your employer doesn't offer a 401(k) plan and you work for a public school, university, hospital, government entity, or other nonprofit organization, check if they provide 403(b) or 457(b) plans instead. These are comparable to 401(k) plans, which are limited to private-sector employers and some nonprofits.

Getting used to reallocating your income like this will take some time, but automating your contributions will free you up, both mentally and logistically. You can take even further advantage of your momentum by contributing to an after-tax investment account as soon as your income can support it. Building passive income is the key to unlocking financial freedom and reducing stress, because it will keep growing without taking time out of your day-to-day. Now, let's dig into the details.

The Power of Momentum and Market Returns

We know the historical annual return of the S&P 500 is about 10 percent a year. Even though past performance isn't indicative of future returns, it's still worthwhile to familiarize yourself with historical data points. Some investment houses, such as Goldman Sachs, Vanguard, and JP Morgan predict that the performance of the S&P 500 over the next one to two decades could be notably lower than the historical average.* But no one knows the future. Strategists make inaccurate forecasts and change their predictions all the time.

Investing in a low-cost S&P 500 exchange-traded fund, or ETF, like SPY or IVV, or an index fund like VTSAX (which stands for Vanguard Total Stock Market Index Fund), is the easiest way to gain exposure. We also know that roughly 70 percent of the time, the S&P 500 performs positively for the year. Therefore, once you build a $250,000 investment portfolio, you have a decent chance of returning roughly $25,000 a year.

Why is $25,000 a year significant? Because it creates both a formidable safety net and the opportunity to earn more passive investment income. At the time of this book's publication, a $25,000 return surpasses the 401(k) contribution limit for employees under fifty years old. When you can potentially make more from your investments than the maximum 401(k) employee contribution for the year, you've got yourself a powerful portfolio to build upon.

This represents a turning point in your wealth-building journey. You can use this accomplishment to motivate yourself to save, invest, and contribute even more. One day, in addition to potentially returning $25,000 a year from your portfolio, you could also

---

* financialsamurai.com/low-stock-market-return-scenario

contribute an equal amount to grow your retirement portfolio by more than $50,000 a year.

Market Returns Plus Maximum 401(k) Contributions

Let's imagine for a moment that you begin maxing out your 401(k) at age twenty-five—a solid milestone in and of itself. You contribute $23,000 a year for eight years and earn a reasonable 7 percent annual rate of return.* Voilà! At the age of thirty-three, your 401(k) will have grown to $252,494.

Your 401(k) balance would be even greater at thirty-three if you started contributing when you were twenty-two, twenty-three, or twenty-four. But you were likely busy paying down student loan debt and trying to make ends meet.

Now let's imagine that, after eight years of below-historical-average growth, the stock market enters a bull market. Instead of earning a 7 percent annual rate of return, from age thirty-three your portfolio earns a 10 percent annual rate of return for the next ten years. Meanwhile, you continue to contribute $23,000 a year for those ten years. How much would you have when you are forty-three?

Plugging the numbers into a simple compound-interest calculator reveals your $252,494 portfolio would have grown to $1,058,121! In just ten short years, your portfolio would have more than quadrupled in value. Your annual contributions accounted for $414,000 ($23,000 × 18 years), or 39 percent of your total $1,058,121. This means that an impressive $644,121—61 percent of your total portfolio—came purely from returns, growing while you did nothing at all. Now that's the power of momentum.

---

* The IRS 401(k) maximum contribution for employees under fifty in 2024 is $23,000 and is subject to change. Check the IRS website for the latest limit.

The Larger Your Portfolio, the Greater the Momentum

As your portfolio grows, it gains momentum.

To illustrate the point further, plug $1,058,121 into a compound-interest calculator. Assume continued annual contributions of $23,000 for ten more years at a 10 percent annual compound rate of return. By the time you're fifty-three, your 401(k) would have grown to $3,147,710, making you a verified multimillionaire! Even with no annual contributions between the ages of forty-three and fifty-three, your $1,058,121 would have grown to $2,744,493 assuming a 10 percent annual compound rate of return. In such a scenario, your contributions of $414,000 between the ages of twenty-five and forty-three now account for just 15 percent of your $2,744,493 portfolio.

Once you build a large enough financial nut, you can create perpetual momentum and accrue wealth automatically.

$250,000 Is the Crossover Point

If you want to become a millionaire, make it your first mission to save and invest as aggressively as possible to build a $250,000 investment portfolio. Draw a big circle around this milestone, because it's one of the most important. Once you get to $250,000, you've reached the crossover point at which your potential returns may regularly exceed the maximum 401(k) contribution amounts.

The crossover point is equal to about ten times the maximum 401(k) contribution limit. And ten times is the inverse of 10 percent—the historical average return of the S&P 500 index. In other words, if the maximum employee contribution to a 401(k) per year increases to $30,000 in the future, the crossover point will then rise to $300,000.

The vast majority of people maxing out their 401(k)s will reach the crossover point within eleven years, based on contributions alone. However, once you assume a reasonable rate of return, the $250,000 crossover point can be reached sooner. If you want to become a millionaire sooner, start maxing out your 401(k) and contributing to taxable investment accounts, real estate, and other risk assets sooner. You will be surprised by how quickly a $250,000 portfolio can turn into more than $1 million.

There are many people who forgo growing passive income and work a nine-to-five until they're sixty. Adopting the *Financial Samurai* way of maxing out your 401(k) as long as you possibly can—and making it an automatic annual milestone—will ensure that you'll become a 401(k) millionaire by a traditional retirement age. Fifty-nine and a half is when you can withdraw funds from your 401(k) without a 10 percent penalty.

For those who would like to achieve FIRE (Financial Independence, Retire Early), reaching the $250,000 crossover point is also the rough start of Coast FIRE, a subtype of FIRE defined as a level of financial independence at which you may no longer have to contribute to your retirement portfolio because it has grown large enough to fund a traditional retirement based on historical returns, thus you can coast to FIRE. Although achieving Coast FIRE sounds nice, don't get lulled into complacency. You won't be truly financially independent, because your investments are unlikely to cover your basic living expenses. Thus, even after your portfolio reaches an amount that could grow to the size you need when you retire, don't stop contributing. The only way to comfortably retire before sixty is to build a large enough taxable portfolio that generates enough investment income to cover your living expenses. I recommend viewing Coast FIRE as a way to appreciate how far you've come, but push further to achieve true financial independence.

401(k) Employer Match Accelerates Growth

According to a survey by Plan Sponsor Council of America, a typical employer matches an employee's contributions to a 401(k) up to 6 percent of that employee's salary. In other words, if an employee earns $50,000, most employers will match up to $3,000. That $3,000 employer match is essentially free money. Taking advantage of a company match for your 401(k), if you have access to one, will accelerate your path to millionaire status.

The example in the previous sections describes a twenty-five-year-old who contributes $23,000 a year to their 401(k) and builds a $252,494 portfolio in eight years after earning a 7 percent annual compound return. If that person's employer matched $5,000 a year, on average, the employee would have a $259,274 portfolio in seven years.

Getting to the $250,000 crossover point a year earlier is significant. Please take full advantage of your company's 401(k) program. Employer contributions are an invaluable tool for building your wealth passively, which you should calculate in the opportunity cost of leaving your job, and its benefits, when you are considering a career change. During the last three years that I worked in banking, my firm contributed between $20,000 and $25,000 a year to my 401(k). Leaving my job at age thirty-four, in 2012, easily cost me more than $300,000 in employer 401(k) contributions alone over ten years.

Find the Motivation to Max Out Every Year

Perhaps some of you are wondering how on earth you'll be able to comfortably max out your 401(k) every year and not be forced to live off delicious rice and beans every day. For some of you, eating frugally and cutting costs to the bare minimum for several years is exactly what it will take.

You really only have to "sacrifice" for the first eleven years of your working career, at most. In eleven years, you will reach the crossover point from your contributions alone. Your actual sacrifice is likely to be much shorter than eleven years because of positive returns, company matches, and raises you might get during this period.

You must achieve many milestones to become a millionaire, and you'll need a lot of discipline. But, compared to staying fit by eating right and exercising regularly as you age, which requires your active, daily engagement, automatically contributing to your 401(k) with each paycheck takes no engagement at all. All you have to do is calculate what percentage of each paycheck is required to max out your 401(k) for the year and commit. The rest is handled by the investments.

For example, if you earn $80,000, and the maximum 401(k) contribution is $24,000, simply elect for your firm to contribute 30 percent of every paycheck directly to your 401(k). It may sound like a lot, but contributions are made with pretax dollars. This means you're losing less in cash flow than what is being contributed to your 401(k).

Let's say you pay a 20 percent effective income tax rate, and your biweekly gross pay is $3,333. A 30 percent pretax contribution to your 401(k) equals $1,000, leaving you with taxable income of $2,333 and an after-tax amount of $1,866.

$3,333	Biweekly gross pay
$1,000	30 percent pretax 401(k) contribution = $3,333 × 30 percent
$2,333	Taxable income = $3,333 - $1,000
$1,866	After-tax take-home pay = $2,333 - $467*

*20 percent effective tax on $2,333

Now let's say you do not contribute anything to your 401(k). Your $3,333 gross pay would be fully taxed at 20 percent, leaving you with $2,666. Sure, you would have $800 more in after-tax income ($2,666 vs. $1,866), but you would lose out on $1,000 in pretax contributions to your 401(k). In other words, contributing $1,000 to your 401(k) automatically increases your net worth by $200 from the time of your contribution until you eventually start taking distributions in retirement.

Once you automate your 401(k) contributions, you will learn to live within your new income. Hedonic adaptation works both ways. Just like how we easily adapt to earning more money, we also easily adapt to earning less.

Fight like hell to get to the $250,000 milestone crossover point. Once you're past it, stay consistent with your maximum contributions and watch your wealth snowball.

How to Save If You Don't Have a 401(k)

If you have a 401(k) or a Roth IRA and decide to withdraw funds before the age of fifty-nine and a half, be aware that the IRS will typically impose a 10 percent penalty.* However, if your $250,000 portfolio is in a taxable brokerage account, you can always draw down principal to pay for some of your living expenses without incurring penalties.

A 4 percent to 5 percent withdrawal rate equals $10,000 to $12,500, enough for some single people to survive a spartan lifestyle. However, with a $250,000 portfolio, there's likely a greater than 50 percent chance it could return more than $25,000 in any

---

* Rule 72(t) enables some people to withdraw from their 401(k) or IRA five years earlier, as I explain here: financialsamurai.com/rule-72t-to-withdraw-money-penalty-free-from-ira-for-early-retirement. Withdrawals from Roth IRAs can also be made tax-free and without the 10 percent penalty in certain situations as described here: schwab.com/ira/roth-ira/withdrawal-rules.

given year given the S&P 500's 10 percent historical average annual return.

Even though there are circumstances where you can withdraw from your taxable portfolio or Roth IRA tax-free and penalty-free, don't. Give your portfolio as much time as possible to compound into the millions. Remember, utilizing momentum is one of the easiest ways to achieve wealth milestones on your way to $1 million and beyond.

As your income grows, you can contribute even more than the 401(k) limit into your taxable brokerage account. This is where maxing out your 401(k) and contributing to your taxable brokerage account creates even more momentum.

If you have the desire to retire early and live off tappable passive income, you must build your taxable portfolio and/or a rental-property portfolio.

Keeping Focus

In retrospect, I should have kept working in finance for five and a half more years, until the age of forty. If I did, I would have been able to save a lot more money. It also would have been nice to get paid parental leave. Alas, I was burned out, and the severance package I negotiated paid for up to six years of my living expenses. So, I figured, why not take a leap of faith.

Nobody retires early from a job they like or love. This is one of my key points in my now-classic post, "The Dark Side of Early Retirement."* Some wandering souls simply haven't found their ideal job yet. But, instead of continuing to search for meaningful work, they give up early and retire.

---

* financialsamurai.com/the-dark-side-of-early-retirement-risks-dangers

Though the $250,000 benchmark is an important one to keep in mind, don't trick yourself into complacency. The term Coast FIRE was coined to give financial independence seekers motivation, to make them feel good despite still being so far away from their goal. So much about money is psychological.

Do not stop saving and investing once you've reached the $250,000 crossover point. If you truly hate your job, take a sabbatical. Alternatively, find a new position within your firm to breathe new excitement into a stale occupation. Perhaps better yet, negotiate a severance package if your job is negatively affecting your life and find a better role after you attain $250,000. Having money enables you to be pickier with your time.

The Next Goal: Reach the Minimum Investment Threshold

Your next goal is to accumulate enough investments to reach a point where work becomes optional. I call this your minimum investment threshold. To determine your own threshold amount, take the inverse of the historical rate of return of the risk assets you plan to own and multiply it by your gross annual income.

$$\frac{Investment}{Threshold} = \frac{1}{Historical\ Return} \times \frac{Gross\ Annual}{Income}$$

For example, if you earn $100,000 a year and are comfortable investing 100 percent of your retirement portfolio in stocks, you can use the historical 10 percent annual return of the S&P 500 as a guide. The inverse of 10 percent is 10, so multiplying 10 by $100,000 equals $1 million. In other words, once your stock portfolio reaches $1 million, you can consider scaling back at work. This might mean finding a more enjoyable job that pays less, going back to school, or becoming a full-time parent until your youngest attends school full time.

$$\frac{Investment}{Threshold} = \frac{1}{0.10} \times 100,000 = 10 \times 100,000 = 1,000,000$$

On average, stocks, real estate, bonds, and other risk assets have a 75 percent probability of providing a positive return each year. Therefore, when your investments begin to generate more income than your job, work becomes less critical. However, since risk assets can also lose value, it's wise to continue saving and investing even after reaching your minimum investment threshold. Ideally, you should pivot to a job you truly enjoy while continuing to build your wealth.

The beauty of my investment threshold formula is that it can be applied to any type of risk asset you choose to own for retirement. Simply find the asset's historical rate of return, take the inverse, and multiply it by your gross income. Additionally, my formula accounts for inflation since incomes are generally indexed to inflation, and inflation can serve as a tailwind to boost investment returns. To stay ahead of inflation, just recalculate your investment threshold once a year or whenever your income changes.

Once you've accumulated enough investments to make work optional, your life will improve significantly. You won't stress as much about meetings and deadlines, and your boss won't bother you as much. The guilt you feel about using all your vacation days will likely disappear, and you can find relief in knowing that you no longer have to grind as hard for that next raise or promotion either. So, keep saving and investing! You'll feel like you're playing with the house's money.

To Contemplate:

- ☐ If you are new to investing or feel anxious about getting started, remember that, about 70 percent of the time, the S&P 500 performs positively for the year.

- ☐ Build your confidence in investment exposure to the S&P 500 by knowing that history has shown that the probability of a positive investment outcome goes up the longer you hold. Your chances of earning a positive return are roughly 79 percent after five years, 88 percent after ten years, and 100 percent after twenty years.

- ☐ The vast majority of people maxing out their 401(k)s will reach the $250,000 crossover point within eleven years based on contributions alone.

To Do:

- ☐ Cut your million-dollar goal down into smaller, digestible amounts. For example, start with a goal to save and invest $10,000 to $20,000 in one year. Smaller savings goals that are easier to reach will give you the motivation to keep going.

- ☐ Work and save like mad to get to $250,000, the crossover point at which you start feeling financially free. Once you get to $250,000, your 401(k) portfolio may begin to regularly return more than you can contribute.

- ☐ Find out what your employer's maximum 401(k) match is and contribute at least that amount. It's free money.

- ☐ Start maxing out your 401(k) as soon as possible and don't stop contributing.

- ☐ Invest in a low-cost S&P 500 ETF like SPY or IVV, or an index fund like VTSAX. The majority of active fund managers underperform their funds' benchmark indices over time.

- [ ] As soon as you have excess cash after maxing out your 401(k), contribute to a taxable brokerage account. Your taxable brokerage account is what will enable you to retire early or take a sabbatical, if you wish.

- [ ] Calculate your minimum investment threshold amount where work becomes optional. Once you achieve this milestone, you will be freer to do what you want.

- [ ] If you want to retire early, grow your portfolio until it generates enough passive income to cover 100 percent of your annual basic living expenses. Just remember that, over time, inflation will eat into your buying power if you stop contributing.

Embrace the Joy of Saving and Investing

IF THE AMOUNT OF MONEY you're saving each month doesn't hurt, you're not saving enough. Anybody who has ever had braces can tell you how uncomfortable they are. From the jolting jabs of pain when you bite down on something, to wanting to rip your teeth out of what feels like a vise grip from hell, you wonder when the torture will end. But it takes discomfort, time, and patience for teeth to straighten. The same philosophy applies to saving money. To make any meaningful headway in accumulating greater wealth, you must experience discomfort, sacrifice, and stay the course.

The percentage of your total income that you save after covering expenses is known as your personal saving rate. It should be high enough that you need to taper down your spending habits, review your budget, and strive to earn more.

Save, Invest, Strain, Repeat

To become a millionaire, you must adopt the fundamental habit of saving as much as possible—until it's uncomfortable. If you don't, then you will likely wake up one day, ten years from now, and wonder where all your money went. Once you have a high enough saving rate on autopilot, you can really start to accelerate your net worth and put your money to work.

Job security and traditional pensions are increasingly becoming relics of the past for many workers. That makes it more important than ever to prioritize your long-term financial stability, no matter what phase of life you are in. There's no time for laziness, procrastination, or overspending. You hold the sole authority to manage your spending habits, enhance your savings, and make wiser career choices. It's time to confront fear head-on and harness the power of compounding and time to your advantage. Too many people wing it when it comes to their personal finances. I want you to be intentional.

It's this intentionality that will get you the financial gains that you want. Those who feel like they're entitled to wealth, without making the necessary sacrifices or putting in the work, are the ones who burn out too quickly to reap the rewards.

Nobody Was Going to Save Me

I realized a month after beginning work at Goldman Sachs that I couldn't last in banking for the rest of my career. The hours were brutal, and the stress was immense. But this was the life I chose to live. I either had to suck it up or get out. As a result, I made the conscious decision to save as much money as possible to give myself the option of leaving work behind someday.

First, I increased my saving rate by sharing a studio apartment with my high school buddy for the first year, then sharing a different studio featuring a windowless alcove with a colleague for my second. I was hardly ever home anyway. Why pay more rent than I had to?

Then, to save money on food, I worked past seven p.m. every evening to gain access to the free corporate cafeteria food at 85 Broad Street. (I may or may not have brought food home for leftovers.) In terms of nights out, unless the firm was taking us analysts out for free drinks, I would pre-party at home on cheap beer before going out, to skip the $10-plus cocktails.

In the end, I ended up saving more than 50 percent of my $40,000 annual salary simply by saving each biweekly paycheck plus my discretionary bonus. It was frugal living, but the habit of saving aggressively stuck with me even decades later.

I wanted to be a multimillionaire by age forty, so I took the easiest route I could find to help me get there: I raised my saving rate.

No One Cares About Your Excuses

Before the pandemic, *Financial Samurai* reader Frank emailed me to say he couldn't save more than 10 percent of his after-tax income each year. He was upset at my net worth– and savings-target charts and said I was "out of touch with reality." I often get this type of feedback from those who aren't willing to put in the effort to outperform themselves financially.

But everything changed for Frank once the pandemic hit. He found himself taking the same steps I did to cut costs. He asked his girlfriend of three years, Elena, to move in with him to create a "pandemic pod" (and to split the cost of rent fifty-fifty). Elena was paying $2,400 a month for her studio. By joining forces, they not only saved on rent but also on food, transportation, and entertainment expenses.

During the lockdowns, Frank and Elena saved the money they previously spent going out, and their food and alcohol expenses declined by $500 per month. Once things began to open back up, they chose to ride their bikes instead of drive, which led to another $200 per month in savings. Finally, the couple decided to take side jobs delivering food and running tasks to make an extra $1,000 per month combined.

These choices boosted Frank's saving rate from 10 percent to 50 percent. After keeping up his newfound saving rate of 50 percent for two years, he wrote me another email that said, "once I stopped making excuses for why I couldn't save, that's when the savings began. Thank you."

Don't wait for a crisis to force yourself to change. Make the changes today. Sooner or later, something bad will happen, and when it does, you'll be better prepared. Keep your $250,000 goal in mind and take steps to reduce food, transportation, and living costs, when possible, to jumpstart your journey toward financial wealth accumulation.

The amount you save hinges on your level of determination to achieve millionaire status. If you choose to embrace a You Only Live Once (YOLO) mindset today, because tomorrow isn't guaranteed, that's understandable. Just be prepared to have less wealth in the future than you initially anticipated.

Thinking about how much money you feel entitled to won't put it in the bank. Keeping a strong conviction and actually acting on earning, saving, and investing will.

Saving Rate and Spending Rate

Your saving rate is the most important number you should focus on in regard to personal finance. The higher your saving rate, the greater your chances of becoming a millionaire, and vice versa.

Surprise! Saving Rate and Savings Rate Are Not the Same Thing

One of the most common typos you'll come across in personal finance literature is the mistaken use of the term "savings rate" instead of "saving rate."

Yes, that sneaky extra s, or the lack of it, changes the meaning of each term. So, what's the difference?

Saving rate is the rate at which someone, like yourself, *saves* money. For example, if you have a $100,000 annual salary, and you save $40,000, your personal saving rate is 40 percent.

Savings rate is the interest rate someone *earns* on their savings. If you put the $40,000 you saved from your salary into a 4.0 percent APY savings account, your savings rate is 4.0 percent. That 4.0 percent savings rate will earn you a nice $1,600 in interest income.

Your saving rate is calculated by dividing your disposable income (income minus spending) by your gross income. Then multiply the result by one hundred to get the percentage:

$$Saving\ Rate = \frac{(Income - Spending)}{Income}$$

Conversely, your spending rate is calculated by dividing your total spending by your gross income:

$$Spending\ Rate = \frac{Spending}{Income}$$

If you have a 90 percent spending rate, you have a 10 percent saving rate. They add up to equal 100 percent. Thus, if you only have a 40 percent spending rate, you have an impressive 60 percent saving rate. This is helpful when you're asking yourself whether it's easier to save more money or spend less. Both acts are different sides of the same coin. Each is a side effect of the other. Understanding their interdependency will help keep your money habits in check as you work toward achieving one financial milestone at a time.

The easiest way to save is to set aside a certain percentage of your income and then spend the rest. You can do so by automatically contributing a certain percentage of your income to a 401(k), IRA, Roth IRA, or taxable brokerage account. By paying yourself first, you won't stress about spending too much of your paycheck (assuming you don't take on consumer debt).

But to really accelerate your saving rate, you must also challenge yourself to spend less money and invest even more after you've set aside a certain percentage for your savings. For those who love spending, trick yourself into viewing your investing as a type of spending. This way, you'll encourage yourself to invest more over time.

The ultimate milestone is to continue raising your saving rate until you can no longer take the pain.

Percentages Are Superior to Flat Dollar Amounts

If you were taught to save a certain dollar amount each month, I want you to toss that old mentality out the window. Replace it with a saving rate percentage. Why? Flat dollar amounts are just that—flat. They are static numbers that won't grow with you over time.

Percentages are better. They eliminate guesswork and reduce financial stress. When your schedule is filled with work and family, using a percentage helps simplify the process of saving more money.

Got a raise? Great! Your saving rate percentage automatically adjusts the dollar amount you're saving each month upward. The same applies if your income goes through a decline due to changing jobs, working fewer hours, getting a divorce, etc. You can also use raises as an opportunity to bump up your saving rate percentage if you are disciplined and keep your expenses the same.

Here's an example. Let's say you currently have a 10 percent saving rate on a posttax salary of $100,000 (saving $10,000, spending $90,000 each year). After beating all your performance objectives, you earn a posttax raise to $110,000. Applying your 10 percent saving rate to $110,000 now brings your annual savings up to $11,000, an additional $1,000 per year. But that also leaves $9,000 of your remaining $10,000 posttax raise up for grabs. If you fight lifestyle inflation by keeping your expenses constant and put that $9,000 into savings, suddenly your saving rate jumps up to 28 percent.

After more years of hard work, let's say you're now earning $150,000 a year posttax. If you continue to live on $90,000 a year, your saving rate jumps to 40 percent ($60,000 / $150,000). Now every year, saving 40 percent of your posttax income brings you nearly one additional year of financial freedom. To build wealth faster, increase your saving rate and keep your living expenses steady—or even lower them—after each raise. Investing more for your future will help you reach your financial goals faster.

Your Target Saving Rate

If you've never tested the limits of your saving, now is the time.

To come up with a reasonable target saving rate, you must first understand what the average saving rate is in your country. Given that you want to be a millionaire, your goal is to thoroughly trounce the average saving rate.

According to data from the Federal Reserve Bank of St. Louis, the average personal saving rate in the United States in 2024 was below 3.5 percent. Compare that to the 1960s through the 1980s, when the average personal saving rate in the US hovered around 10 percent.

Let's put that into perspective. At a 5 percent saving rate, a typical American would need to save for about twenty years to accumulate enough net worth to cover one year of living expenses. When you're spending 95 percent of your income every year, becoming a millionaire is a pipe dream. The typical American is unable to pay for a $5,000 emergency. With such a low saving rate, it's no surprise the median net worth in America is only about $193,000 and that most Americans will have to work well into their sixties and seventies.

Fear Is a Great Impetus for Saving

Here's the thing: we can all save more if we want to. The COVID-19 pandemic is a clear example. In January 2020, the average personal saving rate in the US was 7.2 percent. By April 2020, it had shot up to an astounding 33.8 percent.

Prior to 2020, my baseline recommendation was for everyone to save at least 20 percent of their after-tax income each month. That way, you would save one year's worth of living expenses every five years. After a forty-year career, roughly by age sixty, you would have saved at least eight years' worth of living expenses, which would provide a sufficient buffer before collecting Social Security.

Now, my recommended saving rate is 30 percent or higher. Why? Because there are no more excuses. If you long to become a millionaire, with a net worth more than five times greater than the $193,000 median net worth in America, then you should meet or beat the 30+ percent saving rate the masses managed to save during the pandemic.

Before you start to gripe and groan, focus on the time you'll save. For example, if you increase your saving rate by an additional 10 percent (from 20 percent to 30 percent), you could accumulate at least ten years' worth of living expenses after a thirty-year career (versus eight years after a forty-year career). That's ten fewer years that you'll need to work! How much is an extra ten years of freedom worth to you?

The chart on the following page demonstrates the power of increasing your saving rate.

The minimum saving rate you'll need to be a millionaire is 30 percent. However, once you can get to a 50 percent saving rate, that is when the magic really starts to happen. At that point, you are saving one full year of future living expenses every year.

Always keep in mind that you're not merely saving 30 percent or more of your after-tax income, you're also investing 100 percent of that amount. You are sowing seeds of wealth that will, through compound returns, yield prosperity. As a result, when you decide you no longer wish to work, you'll have the financial freedom you've diligently worked toward.

Financial Freedom Saving Rate Chart

Based on $100,000 in income after tax

Saving Rate	Amount Saved	Annual Expenses	Years to Save 1 Year of Expenses	Years of Living Expenses Saved after 10 Years	Years of Living Expenses Saved after 20 Years	Years of Living Expenses Saved after 30 Years
5%	$5,000	$95,000	19.00	0.53	1.05	1.58
10%	$10,000	$90,000	9.00	1.11	2.22	3.33
15%	$15,000	$85,000	5.67	1.76	3.53	5.29
20%	$20,000	$80,000	4.00	2.50	5.00	7.50
25%	$25,000	$75,000	3.00	3.33	6.67	10.00
30%	$30,000	$70,000	2.33	4.29	8.57	12.86
35%	$35,000	$65,000	1.86	5.38	10.77	16.15
40%	$40,000	$60,000	1.50	6.67	13.33	20.00
45%	$45,000	$55,000	1.22	8.18	16.36	24.55
50%	$50,000	$50,000	1.00	10.00	20.00	30.00
55%	$55,000	$45,000	0.82	12.22	24.44	36.67
60%	$60,000	$40,000	0.67	15.00	30.00	45.00
65%	$65,000	$35,000	0.54	18.57	37.14	55.71
70%	$70,000	$30,000	0.43	23.33	46.67	70.00
75%	$75,000	$25,000	0.33	30.00	60.00	90.00
80%	$80,000	$20,000	0.25	40.00	80.00	120.00
85%	$85,000	$15,000	0.18	56.67	113.33	170.00
90%	$90,000	$10,000	0.11	90.00	180.00	270.00

Assumptions: 1) Start work after high school or college; 2) 0 percent returns; 3) Investment income kicks in after retirement; 4) Social Security kicks in by age seventy; 5) Grey boxes show when you can retire; 6) Focus on the years, not the income.

Source: FinancialSamurai.com

THE *FINANCIAL SAMURAI* WAY

To Contemplate:

☐ Think about your most common excuses for not saving and investing more and how they are holding you back from greater wealth.

☐ Reflect on any pain points and sacrifices you've made for the benefit of your finances.

To Do:

☐ Make a pact with yourself that you are willing to sacrifice to save more money and accumulate greater wealth. Dig deep. To strengthen your resolve, revisit the motivations for gaining wealth that you wrote down earlier.

☐ Switch from using a flat, inflexible saving methodology to a dynamic one using percentages.

☐ Calculate your monthly disposable income (income minus spending).

☐ Use your calculated monthly disposable income to determine your current personal saving rate by dividing it by your monthly gross income. Then multiply the result by one hundred to get the percentage.

☐ Challenge yourself to boost your saving rate to 30 percent, the target rate if you want to be a millionaire by sixty. To get there, increase your saving rate percentage by 1–2 percent per month. Once you get to 30 percent, keep going. At a 50 percent saving rate, every year you save equals one year of freedom.

Build Net Worth for Security and Cash Flow for Life

I THOUGHT MY INCOME WAS going to reach make-it-rain status by 2017, the year I turned forty. Alas, the 2008–09 downturn slashed my income in half. It recovered in 2010 and 2011, but when I left the finance industry in 2012, my income decreased by 80 percent.

With a much lower income, I had to cut spending aggressively. However, my semiliquid net worth of about $2 million was able to generate about $80,000 a year in passive investment income, which I used to pay for my general living expenses. With a working wife, whose salary could provide liquidity if a serious emergency arose, plus reliable, subsidized health care provided by her employer, I was fine.

It took about three years of working online for my income to reach the same level as my old day job. By then, my wife had joined me in semiretirement after negotiating her own severance at the age of thirty-five. Since my online income was more volatile than my salary at my previous day job, I continued to save and invest to build even more passive income.

Income comes and goes. Net worth is stickier, but the rate at which your net worth grows will shift and change over time. The goal is to have your net worth increase as quickly and as often as possible.

Stay Disciplined If You Want Your Net Worth to Take Off

It's great to focus on supercharging your income. However, what's equally important is figuring out how to reinvest your savings into other asset classes that have a high probability of providing you with a positive return.

Sooner or later, you will not want to work all that hard for your money. When that time comes, you'll hopefully have multiple asset classes working *for you*.

No matter how much money you make, stay disciplined by saving and investing. Your saving rate and net worth should grow as your income does. Ideally, max out your tax-advantaged retirement accounts as soon as possible, then save an additional 20 percent or more of your remaining after-tax income.

Once you hit a net worth equal to ten times your average annual gross income, that is when you'll start feeling the joys of financial freedom. Whether you had a late start in life or are fortunate enough to be making a high income, it's important to stay disciplined and keep on growing your net worth each year. Reference the chart on page 14 in Milestone 1 to get a great idea of where your net worth should be by age.

Reasons to Prioritize Growing Your Net Worth

Growing your net worth requires more oversight than growing your income. Increasing your income is relatively straightforward.

Work hard, gain experience, provide value, job hop for better opportunities, and be a good person—all these things generally lead to higher income levels over time.

Growing your net worth is more complicated. With the wrong asset allocation, you could suffer tremendous losses that set you back a decade. Taking on too much debt or buying stocks on margin (borrowing money from a broker to purchase stocks) could completely wipe out your net worth during a bear market. Ironically, holding too much cash may also make you poorer over time, given the poor performance of cash and the temptation to spend it.

Plenty of people have high incomes, but many of those people are still destined to work forever due to a lack of focus on growing their net worth over time. Luckily, you are not one of these people.

The less you have to rely on active income, the more secure and happier you'll be. Once you're financially independent, everything you do will be because you want to, not because you have to.

Here are some key reasons why it's beneficial to focus on growing your net worth more than your employment income:

1) The government goes after income, not wealth

We have a progressive tax system in America. The more you make, the larger the percentage the government will take away. If you are in the top marginal income tax bracket and live in a place like California, New Jersey, or New York, you will send the government around 50 percent of every dollar earned beyond a certain threshold.

Do you really want to work forty to eighty hours a week only to have the government take away close to half of what you get to keep? I don't. Paying any more than a 24 percent federal marginal income tax rate already seems like too much, and the next tax rate jumps to 32 percent.* Don't forget, you may have to pay state income taxes, city taxes, and FICA taxes as well.

But, if you were single, with no W-2 income, and had $1 million in your investment portfolio generating $40,000 a year, you would owe the government nada, because that $40,000 falls under the zero percent capital gains tax rate. Getting to keep 100 percent of your investment income is wonderful. Imagine what you could do with a $3 million net worth, which generates $120,000 a year in passive income. As a single individual, you'd only have to pay a 15 percent long-term capital gains tax rate versus a 24 percent marginal federal income tax rate if that income had come from a day job instead.†

2) You will develop a long-term wealth mindset

When you focus on making a higher income, you're trading your time for money. But, if you shift your focus to building a million-dollar-plus *net worth*, you can concentrate on growing wealth through investments and business equity without gouging hours out of your day.

The truly wealthy are those with their own businesses or those who have equity stakes in others' businesses. Their net worth grew as their business interests took up a higher percentage of their total net worth. Shareholders of companies think more holistically, and longer term, than income-only employees.

When you set milestones that are focused on building wealth, you will naturally move toward building generational wealth for your descendants. Instead of investing for the next five years, you

---

* Per the IRS's 2024 federal income tax rates and brackets, which are subject to change in subsequent years.
† Based on the IRS's 2024 long-term capital gains tax brackets.

start thinking about investing in real estate or artificial intelligence companies for the next twenty years. Because, if you don't, you know that, twenty years from now, your children will ask why you didn't invest in such assets today. Just think about all the cheap real estate and stocks your grandparents could have gobbled up while they were working.

If you are a parent, it's comforting to be able to set up your children for life in case you pass away prematurely. Of course, you hope your children will become financially independent on their own. But having enough resources to know that everything will be okay once you are gone can provide priceless comfort.

3) Net worth is more easily concealable

Why would you ever want to conceal your true net worth? To provide peace, safety, and privacy for you and your family. Once people know you're rich, they might treat you differently, for better or for worse. They might also target you for money.

Net worth can be spread across many different companies and investments. As a result, it's much harder to calculate one's true net worth than one's employment income. For example, you may have twenty-five financial accounts that make up your net worth rather than just one paycheck.

Nosy people can guesstimate a portion of your net worth through visible holdings, like your primary residence or car. But it's impossible for someone to figure out your entire net worth if you practice Stealth Wealth. As a Financial Samurai, your goal is to get rich without other people noticing.

There will always be some level of disdain for the wealthy. Protecting your family and your mental health is one of the benefits of having a high net worth that generates passive income, rather than a high income from working in an often-vilified industry.

4) Less temptation to spend irresponsibly

Typically, employment income is paid biweekly. Each time you get an injection of income, you may have a resulting desire to spend it.

Receiving a high income is akin to walking into your kitchen after not eating all day and seeing a tray full of freshly baked cookies sitting on the kitchen counter. Only the most disciplined will be able to resist eating them! With a high income, you sometimes can't help but buy a bunch of things you don't need until your house is filled with clutter.

Net worth is more complicated and much less liquid than income. You can't just decide to sell a rental property tomorrow to pay for a bender with your friends in Vegas. Selling a property typically requires at least one month of preparation, at least a couple of weeks to find a buyer, and another month to close escrow. Early withdrawals from a CD often have early withdrawal penalties. Meanwhile, private funds often have a five-to-ten-year vesting period. Stocks and certain bonds can be sold quickly, but, even still, it usually takes three business days for the proceeds to hit your bank account. The ease of selling stocks and bonds is part of the reason why most individual investors underperform long-term index-fund investors.

Think about your net worth as a vault where it's easy to deposit funds but it's hard to withdraw. The longer you can keep your money in the vault, the wealthier you will be.

5) A greater feeling of security

The feeling of security might be the best reason to focus on building a large net worth instead of building a large income stream. Everybody's number is different, but I promise you will feel more secure once you reach your net worth target than you will once you reach your income target number. Income comes and goes. If properly managed, however, net worth is forever. A stable net worth that perpetually generates passive income can set you and your family up for life. The key is to reduce risk once you've reached your target net worth.

For example, at one point after the Fed tightened interest rates post-pandemic, investors could buy thirty-year Treasury bonds yielding 5-plus percent risk-free while inflation was at 3.5 percent. If you built a million-dollar net worth that generated $50,000-plus for thirty years, wouldn't you feel secure? Very few jobs provide thirty years of security. Our energy and our opportunities simply run out.

Set a milestone to reach a net worth large enough that you can live on just your investment income and never touch the principal. Never having to draw down principal creates generational wealth for your family.

Become More Conservative Over Time

The larger your net worth, the more confident you will feel about your finances. However, just like how growth stocks can quickly lose a tremendous amount of their value, it's dangerous to be overly confident about your net worth figure.

The closer you are to your target net worth—presumably an amount you feel comfortable living on for the rest of your life—the more conservative you should be. The last thing you want is for a bear market to wipe out 20 to 50 percent of your net worth a few short years into your retirement.

Take a look at the table on the following page, which depicts the conventional asset-allocation model for stocks and bonds by age. In a two-asset class portfolio, the bond allocation percentage follows your age. Historically, but not always, bonds have provided less downside risk than stocks. Therefore, your net worth should have a lower chance of shrinking during difficult times with a larger bond allocation.

The Proper Asset Allocation of Stocks and Bonds by Age

Conventional Model

Age	Stocks	Bonds
0-25	100%	0%
30	70%	30%
35	65%	35%
40	60%	40%
45	55%	45%
50	50%	50%
55	45%	55%
60	40%	60%
65	35%	65%
70	30%	70%
75+	25%	75%

Source: FinancialSamurai.com

For more asset allocation models for stocks and bonds, see financialsamurai.com/the-proper-asset -allocation-of-stocks-and-bonds-by-age.

Of course, there are more asset classes to invest in than just stocks and bonds. The main alternative is real estate, which I cover in Milestone 6. You may consider real estate a bond-plus type of investment. The word *plus* here means that real estate is a type of bond that has more upside potential and less downside potential. Real estate and bonds act similarly. When interest rates go down, both bond and real estate values tend to go up. When interest rates go up, their values tend to go down, but not always.

Personally, I invested more heavily in real estate than in bonds during my career. As a young man in my twenties and thirties, I had the energy and risk tolerance to invest more money into an asset class that provided shelter, generated income, and was improvable through remodeling. Now, as a father with two young children, I've slowed my investments in physical real estate given my lack of desire to manage rental properties. Time is more precious to me now, and as such, I'm more particular about how I use it.

Here is a snapshot of my net worth breakdown, excluding my online business assets. These percentages will undoubtedly change over time, but they are more or less at my target asset-allocation percentages based on my risk tolerance and goals. In general, I do not recommend having any one asset class take up more than 50 percent of your net worth due to concentration risk.

- 50 percent of my net worth is in real estate (including my primary home)
- 25 percent is in dividend-paying stocks (including the S&P 500)
- 15 percent is in growth stocks (no dividends)
- 5 percent is in municipal bonds and Treasury bonds
- 5 percent is in venture capital (private growth companies)

In other words, about 80 percent of my net worth is in lower-volatility investments that generate cash flow. The remaining 20 percent of my net worth is invested in growth stocks and venture capital that does not generate steady income. If I were to need more income, I could simply shift my growth-stock allocation to real estate, dividend-paying stocks, or bonds.

Like a director in a movie, you have the ability to mold your net worth to your vision.

Other Ways to Boost Cash Flow (Income)

Given how important cash flow is, how can you increase it? Here are some suggestions.

- Allocate more capital toward higher-yielding investments. Treasury bonds yielding more than 5 percent are one example; another is NOBL, an ETF that tracks the S&P 500 Dividend Aristocrats (high-quality companies with stable earnings that have paid increasing dividends for twenty-five or more years consecutively).

- Boost work output and efficiency to increase your pay at your existing employer.

- Job hop to a competitor for an immediate pay raise.

- Take a second full-time job if you work from home (may require clandestine behavior if not allowed by your primary employer).

- Do some consulting part time.

- Increase rents on your properties to bring them closer to market levels, if you haven't done so in a while.

- Expand or remodel a property to generate more rental income.

- Invest in bonds and income funds, especially when rates are higher.

- Start a side hustle, or many.

- Create a new product you can sell online or in person.

- Consult or give private lessons based on your expertise.

- Be a hard-money lender.

A high-interest-rate environment is a positive for those who want to generate more cash flow. For example, a 5 percent interest rate can generate $5,000 a year in income on $100,000, while a 2 percent interest rate can only generate $2,000. Focus on being a saver, investor, and lender, not a spender, in a high-interest-rate environment.

Conversely, in a low-interest-rate environment, focus on investing in riskier assets for potentially higher returns. Given that the opportunity cost of earning risk-free income is lower in a low-interest-rate environment, you can afford to take more risk.

In other words, for illustrative purposes, let's say a bond is yielding 20 percent risk-free in a high-interest-rate environment. The opportunity cost of not owning that bond is high because you would be forsaking 20 percent risk-free. Therefore, you would be reticent to invest your cash in risk assets like stocks unless you believed they would return far greater than 20 percent. You would require a risk premium over the 20 percent guaranteed rate of return to account for potential losses. But if a bond was only yielding 2 percent risk-free in a low-interest-rate environment, the opportunity cost of not owning that bond is low. Based on the average annual historical stock market return of 10 percent, the bond's 2 percent guaranteed rate of return is relatively less appealing. If you're still on the path to financial independence, you'd be better off investing in the stock market or any other asset that is expected to yield more than 2 percent.

Date Your Income, Marry Your Net Worth

Sooner or later, your active income will leave you. Do your best to keep as much of it as possible. In good times, when income is high, stay disciplined by raising your saving rate. When times are bad, slash your spending in order to maintain as high a saving rate as possible.

Aim to build as large a net worth as possible to generate as much passive income as you can to support your lifestyle. Treat it as your enduring foundation, not vulnerable to age or health. Guard and grow your wealth wisely through life's ups and downs, and think in terms of decades and generations to come.

Your net worth is for life. Grow it responsibly.

THE *FINANCIAL SAMURAI* WAY

To Contemplate:

☐ Shift your focus from making a higher income to building a million-dollar (or greater) net worth.

☐ Expand your wealth mindset to think more holistically and longer term about your investments, like entrepreneurs and shareholders do. Don't just think five years out, make it twenty.

☐ Don't get tricked by an overinflated net worth during good times. Remember that cash flow is real, but net worth is subjective—it can vary greatly depending on its composition. Who is to say your Picasso is worth the $10 million you think it is? Only when you sell the painting will the market determine its real value.

To Do:

☐ Work toward a net worth equal to ten times your average annual gross income to achieve a degree of financial freedom. Once there, stay disciplined by saving and investing more to eventually get to a net worth equal to twenty times your gross income.

☐ Study the differences between the federal marginal income tax brackets and the federal capital gains tax brackets for your current and future expected annual income. Notice that the government goes after income more than wealth.

☐ Adopt Stealth Wealth to conceal your true net worth for greater privacy, safety, and peace.

☐ Boost your cash flow with higher-yielding investments, a side hustle, job hopping for a pay raise, and other tactics.

☐ Maximize your income while you're still able. Income opportunities don't last forever, but your net worth can.

Accelerate Your Wealth with Real Estate

OWNING YOUR PRIMARY RESIDENCE IS one of the key milestones that will help you become a millionaire. Inflation, rental-income growth, asset-price appreciation, and responsibly borrowing money at a reasonable rate are powerful forces that can help make you rich with minimal active work. For hundreds of years, real estate has built tremendous wealth for millions of everyday people, and it will do the same for you if you invest smartly. There's a reason why practically every millionaire you meet owns real estate. The asymmetric risk and reward of real estate makes it a favorable asset class to build wealth.

Real Estate: A Key Variable for My Financial Freedom

I attribute my early retirement from finance, at age thirty-four, to my investments in real estate. When I left my day job, I had roughly $80,000 in annual investment income, $36,000 of which came from one rental property—a median-priced condo that I lived in for only two years before renting it out. Sure, there were turnover and maintenance issues here and there. Don't remind me about the time the shower leaked into the unit below. But, for the most part, the condo has been a steady engine of income that has provided me with a basic level of financial security. I paid off the mortgage by 2015 and continue to rent it out today.

Once I recognized the wealth-building power of real estate, I was hooked. I bought another property in 2005, this time a single-family home, and lived in it until 2014. Although I experienced dicey times during the 2008 global financial crisis, I ultimately was able to improve the quality of my life during that ten-year period. After that, I rented out the house for three years for about $5,000 a month, after expenses.

During that time, the house was rented to a revolving group of five guys in their twenties and early thirties, who frequently threw parties, damaged the place, paid rent late, and caused disturbances. So, no, being a landlord is not always smooth sailing. I had intended to keep the house for longer, but I sold it when my son was born, in 2017. As a first-time dad full of stress and anxiety, I wanted to minimize the time I spent being a landlord and maximize my time with my boy. The house sold for 80 percent more than I paid for it, and I reinvested the proceeds in stocks, bonds, and a private real estate fund for 100 percent passive income.

There will come a time in every real estate investor's life when they need to decide whether the hassle of being a landlord is worth the returns. As you get older, busier, and wealthier, a readjustment of your investments may be in order. However, the growth of private real estate opportunities online has made investing in real estate 100 percent passive, if you so choose. In the past, regular people would only be able to invest in publicly traded real estate investment trusts (REITs) or real estate ETFs, which were often more volatile than the S&P 500. But the 2012 JOBS Act eased restrictions on real estate syndication platforms, enabling investors to diversify more easily into private real estate of all types across the country.

Be on the Right Side of the Government and Inflation

The power of real estate lies in its asymmetric risk and reward. Given that the government provides subsidies in the form of mortgage-interest tax deductions, up to $250,000 in capital gains tax exclusions on profits when you sell your primary residence ($500,000 for married couples),* and occasional bailouts for over-extended homeowners, you'd be unwise not to invest in real estate.

Be on the government's side as much as possible. You should not only follow its tax laws but also utilize every tax benefit related to real estate ownership that you can. Real estate is also a long-term beneficiary of inflation. As inflation increases, so do rents and property values. After all, housing is also a part of the Consumer Price Index (CPI).

In an inflationary environment, you want to own property with a fixed-rate mortgage. As inflation picks up, the cost of the mortgage declines in real dollars. Meanwhile, the principal value of the home tends to increase with inflation. This one-two combination is one of the reasons why the average homeowner is forty times wealthier than the average renter.

Not only is real estate a beneficiary of inflation, but it is also a hedge against inflation. Let's say inflation zooms much higher than expected due to some unexpected exogenous variable. If you

---

* Qualifications include owning and living in the property as your primary residence for two or more of the five years prior to its date of sale. See more at irs.gov/taxtopics /tc701.

own real estate, either with a mortgage or outright, your living costs will stay more or less the same. You're hedged against rising costs while your property increases in value.

On the other hand, if you are a renter, you are at the mercy of inflation. In economic terms, you are a price taker, not a price determiner. If inflation is accelerating, your chance of facing a rent increase also rises. At the very least, most landlords will pass on rising property and maintenance costs to their tenants. At the very worst, some landlords might want to maximize profits by raising rents as much as allowable when demand for rent significantly exceeds supply.

The best economic environment for a renter is a deflationary one in which prices are falling. However, history has shown that inflation is largely an unstoppable force. In the past sixty years, according to the St. Louis Fed, the United States has only experienced deflation twice: in 2009, with the Great Recession, and in 2015, when the CPI barely broke below zero percent at −0.1 percent.

Be on the right side of the government and inflation. It makes becoming a millionaire much easier.

Why Real Estate Is a Favorite Asset Class of the Wealthy

There's a reason why every rich person you know owns multiple properties. It's the same reason that enormous fortunes have been made through real estate: asymmetric risk and reward.

When it comes to making money, if there is no risk, there is usually very little reward. The biggest reason for the widening wealth gap is ownership in real estate or a lack thereof. Renters in major US cities can spend upward of $2.5 million in rent over the course of their lifetimes. That should make you feel queasy. Just like it's unwise to short the S&P 500 long term, it's unwise to short the real estate market by renting long term.

Lifetime Rent in Five Most Expensive Cities

City	1-bedroom median rent	Amount Paid by Age 30	Amount Paid by Age 40	Amount Paid by Age 50	Amount Paid by Age 60
New York, NY	$4,040	$565,967	$1,329,656	$2,360,143	$3,750,634
Jersey City, NJ	$3,220	$451,092	$1,059,775	$1,881,104	$2,989,366
Boston, MA	$3,000	$420,272	$987,368	$1,752,581	$2,785,124
San Francisco, CA	$2,950	$413,268	$970,912	$1,723,371	$2,738,705
Miami, FL	$2,690	$376,844	$885,340	$1,571,481	$2,497,328

Assumptions: Starting age is twenty. Annual 3 percent increase. Calculations are approximate.

Sources: FinancialSamurai.com, Zumper.com

With homeownership, you have a *chance* to build wealth through home equity. Factors such as natural disasters and rising insurance rates may negatively affect those chances, but real estate gives you a high likelihood of earning a positive return on your investment over time. For reference, the annualized average growth rate of the US housing market for the past four decades has been between 4 and 10 percent, depending on the source and inputs used.

In most worst-case scenarios, as long as a homeowner continues to pay their mortgage, even if the home does not appreciate in value, they can build wealth through forced savings. With a principal-and-interest mortgage, a portion of each payment goes toward paying down principal and the rest to interest. Over time, the mortgage balance declines, the payment stays fixed, and a larger and larger portion of that payment goes toward principal. This type of forced savings builds home equity and keeps homeowners disciplined each month. Renters also have the option to force themselves to save and invest each month. However, when investing in risk assets is not forced or automatic, it's easy to spend money on frivolous things that do nothing to build your net worth.

Once you've paid off your home, its full value is 100 percent a part of your net worth. You can live in the home rent-free, which is the true value of owning a paid-off home, rent out the home for semi-passive income, or pass the home on to your children.

My First Property

When I bought my first condo, in early 2003, I put 20 percent down on $580,000. My mortgage payment was roughly $2,400 a month at 5.75 percent interest. I had just turned twenty-six and was nervous, but I was adamant about not paying more than $2,000 a month on rent, which was the going rate for comparable rental properties at the time. The $2,400 mortgage payment contributed $500 to principal and $1,900 to interest. After accounting for property taxes and deductions, I realized that the $400 price difference between owning and renting was essentially a wash. This gave me more confidence to buy.

By 2013, long after I'd moved out and started renting out that condo, I had refinanced my mortgage rate down to 3.375 percent on a loan of $285,000 (from $464,000 originally). By that time, I had paid down $179,000 (or 39 percent) of the original principal through regular mortgage payments and occasional extra principal payments.

In the ten years from 2003 to 2013, not only did the mortgage's interest payment drop, from $1,900 to $800 (−58 percent), but the rent I was collecting went up, from $2,000 to $3,600 (+80 percent). Today, the mortgage is zero, because I finally paid the sucker off in 2015. With rent now at $4,600, I'm earning $3,500 in income each month from the condo after expenses and taxes.

Ten Times Greater Home Equity

My 20 percent down payment of $116,100 in 2003 turned into a cool $1.25 million twelve years later with minimal work on my part. Yes, I had to pay property taxes and mortgage interest during this time period. However, the rent I didn't pay crossed off these expenses and then some. During that time, my tenants also helped pay down my principal. All I had to do was find good tenants every two to three years and make sure everything in the condo was in working order.

If I had tried to grow $116,100 into $1,250,000 in twelve years without taking out a mortgage, I would have needed to earn a 22 percent compound annual return in stocks or any other investment for twelve years straight. A 22 percent annual rate of return is possible; however, not even the great Warren Buffett has matched such results. His compound return from 1965 through 2022 was "only" 19.8 percent, resulting in a fortune in excess of $100 billion. Getting to $1,250,000 was possible for me because I borrowed responsibly to purchase real estate. I couldn't have realistically grown my money to that level over twelve years in the stock market. Taking on mortgage debt creates leverage, which boosts returns when asset prices are increasing. Just be careful you don't take on too much debt, as losses are also magnified during downturns.

The beauty of real estate is that it's understandable and easy. While you are busy living in your home and making memories, chances are high you're building wealth in the background. All you have to do is continue paying your bills.

What happens to most homeowners over time is their mortgage debt declines, their property value increases, and, as a result, so does their homeowner's equity.

Even if you don't invest a single dollar in any other asset class, if you buy real estate you should end up with a fully paid-off property that provides some financial security within thirty years. Once your living expenses are covered, life gets much easier. If you can build a diversified net worth, all the better.

Unlike stocks, real estate doesn't lose 30-plus percent of its value overnight due to some slight earnings miss. Real estate values are much steadier, which provides more peace of mind. Ironically, because real estate is less risky than stocks, you can make more money from real estate. Because there is less risk, people are more willing to buy more real estate and incur debt to do so.

Buy Property as Soon as You Possibly Can

Given that time is one of the most important variables to getting rich through real estate, my general recommendation is to buy property as soon as you possibly can.

Think about all the times you've heard your grandparents talk about how inexpensive things were when they were young. My grandfather, Albert, may he rest in peace, told me he could have bought a 5,000-square-foot lot facing the world-famous Waikiki beach in Honolulu, Hawaii, back in 1950. He was a teacher with a modest income, but he could have afforded the land because it was less than $35,000. He ultimately decided against the purchase, because he couldn't get over the fact that there was a butcher right next door. That land is worth well over $30 million today. Even though he didn't end up buying land in Waikiki, he diligently saved and bought land elsewhere that is worth exponentially more today than when he bought it.

The earlier you buy real estate, the more you can let your returns compound, and the sooner you get to stop fighting housing inflation as well. When we are young, time is on our side. But, once we hit middle age, time starts becoming our enemy. *We lose our enthusiasm and energy the older we get.* When you buy real estate young, you can more easily ride out the cycles. When you're younger, you're also more willing to go through the pains of remodeling and fixing things that are broken.

How to Determine How Much
Home You Can Afford

In order to buy property as soon as you can, you must have a clear vision of what you want to do and where you want to be. To help you determine how big of a price tag you can afford on a home, follow my 30-30-3 home-buying guidelines. Here are its three principles:

Rule #1: Spend no more than 30 percent of your gross income on a monthly mortgage payment.

Rule #2: Have at least 30 percent of the home value saved up in cash or semiliquid assets so you can put 20 percent down and have a 10 percent buffer.

Rule #3: Limit the total value of your target home to no more than three times your annual household gross income.

You must fulfill at least two of the three rules before purchasing a property. Ideally, you will fulfill all three. Using these rules will prevent premature buying and its resultant buyer's remorse. Unexpected expenses will begin to pop up after your purchase, and that will stress you out or worse if you overextended your finances.

I've put together a handy guide to help you determine how much you can afford based on your income, net worth, and home price. Locate the home price you've set your sights on in the table and make sure you have either 1) the Minimum Income Required paired with the Reasonable Net Worth in that same row or 2) a combination of the Reasonable Income and the Minimum Net Worth Required or better. Ideally, you should have both Reasonable Income and Reasonable Net Worth or better before you dive in headfirst.

Income and Net Worth Necessary to Buy a Home Based on the 30-30-3 Guidelines

Home Price	Minimum Income Required	Reasonable Income	Ideal Income	Minimum Net Worth Required	Reasonable Net Worth	Ideal Net Worth
$200,000	$40,000	$50,000	$66,667	$60,000	$100,000	$666,667
$300,000	$60,000	$75,000	$100,000	$90,000	$150,000	$1,000,000
$400,000	$80,000	$100,000	$133,333	$120,000	$200,000	$1,333,333
$500,000	$100,000	$125,000	$166,667	$150,000	$250,000	$1,666,667
$750,000	$150,000	$187,500	$250,000	$225,000	$375,000	$2,500,000
$1,000,000	$200,000	$250,000	$333,333	$300,000	$500,000	$3,333,333
$1,500,000	$300,000	$375,000	$500,000	$450,000	$1,050,000	$5,000,000
$2,000,000	$400,000	$500,000	$666,667	$600,000	$1,400,000	$6,666,667
$2,500,000	$500,000	$625,000	$833,333	$750,000	$1,750,000	$8,333,333
$3,000,000	$600,000	$750,000	$1,000,000	$900,000	$3,000,000	$10,000,000
$3,500,000	$700,000	$875,000	$1,166,667	$1,050,000	$3,500,000	$11,666,667
$4,000,000	$800,000	$1,000,000	$1,333,333	$1,200,000	$4,000,000	$13,333,333
$4,500,000	$900,000	$1,125,000	$1,500,000	$1,350,000	$4,500,000	$15,000,000
$5,000,000	$1,000,000	$1,250,000	$1,666,667	$1,500,000	$5,000,000	$16,666,667

Minimum Income Required is one-fifth of Home Price; Ideal Income is one-third of Home Price

Minimum Net Worth Required is 30 percent of Home Price; Ideal Net Worth is three and one-third times Home Price

Source: FinancialSamurai.com

Be careful not to underestimate ongoing property taxes, maintenance costs, insurance bills, and repairs. I can tell you from experience that things tend to go bust unexpectedly at the most inconvenient times. The bottom of your hot water heater could rust out and flood your basement while your in-laws are visiting for two weeks. Or you could wake up at two a.m. one morning before a big client meeting to find your roof is leaking. Although the benefits of homeownership largely outweigh the cons, be prepared for abrupt, multi-thousand-dollar repairs and upticks in stress.

If you are older and have a dream home in sight, it may be feasible to spend up to five times your household income on it. However, you must adhere to rules #1 and #2. Failing to do so could lead to excessive stress, undermining your primary reason for buying a nicer home: a better quality of life.

The Main Problem Is Coming Up with the Down Payment

Saving up enough money for a down payment on your first home is a significant milestone, one that is harder than ever in today's world. But don't let that deter you. Remember, you are already ahead of the average person simply by gaining the wealth-building knowledge in this book.

Initially, it's easier to build wealth through stocks, as there is no minimum deposit required. You can buy a single share of a $10 stock to get started. Real estate, on the other hand, has a much higher threshold for entry due to the minimum down payment of 3 percent of the value of the property. A 20 percent down payment is recommended to avoid having to pay for private mortgage insurance.

Buying a historically appreciating asset sooner is generally better for building wealth, but how is a first-time homebuyer supposed to come up with a 3 to 20 percent down payment? The solutions are to save like mad, take out a bigger mortgage, or borrow from the Bank of Mom and Dad. In some cases, all three may be required.

It wasn't always this way. Here's what I've learned from my own observations and countless conversations with real estate agents since 1999. Before 1970, buying a home on a single income was not difficult. Between 1970 and 2010, the need for dual incomes increased. Since 2010, it has become quite commonplace to need dual incomes plus the Bank of Mom and Dad to buy a home. For example, in my hometown of San Francisco, between 30 and 40 percent of first-time homebuyers get down-payment assistance from their parents. The percentages are similar in other high-cost-of-living cities.

With baby boomers sitting on tens of trillions of dollars of wealth, it has become normalized for parents to help their adult children financially. Who wouldn't want to see more joy on their children's faces? I think most would. There is no shame in asking your parents for down-payment assistance, if it doesn't disrupt their financial security. As a parent myself, there is nothing I wouldn't do for my children. If there's a financial case for making the ask, do it. The key is to do so in a respectful way.

A few tips to convince your parents to help out are to maintain regular contact, express your love, and demonstrate your knowledge about real estate and its value. Plan your request well in advance to showcase your level of commitment, work ethic, and recent achievements. The more informed and compelling you are in your pitch for support, the more confidence you can instill in them, and the more motivated they'll be to contribute for mutual fulfillment and happiness.

If your parents are unable, or unavailable, to help you come up with a down payment, don't worry. View your circumstances as an opportunity to succeed. Nothing is more gratifying than being able to depend on yourself as an adult. Let's walk through the steps to get a down payment with a single income.

Median Sales Price of US Homes Sold

Sources: US Census Bureau and US Department of Housing and Urban Development

Establish Clear Targets and Commit

Once you are regularly maxing out your 401(k) or other tax-advantaged accounts, it's time to aggressively build your home-down-payment fund. You must have the same amount of intensity in coming up with a down payment as you do in building a $250,000-plus stock portfolio.

To determine how much to save for a down payment, start with identifying the median home price in the city where you want to buy. Then multiply that by 10 to 20 percent to get a target down-payment range. To illustrate, if the median home price is $500,000, your target down-payment range will be $50,000 to $100,000.

If your target down-payment range is daunting, break it down into smaller annual saving amounts to reduce your anxiety and make it more manageable.

Setting Your Real Estate Goals

To put things in perspective, the typical first-time homebuyer is around thirty-six years old. That gives you eighteen years after high school and fourteen years after college during which you can save for a down payment. If you're older, then you should have a higher income than you did as a new graduate and be able to save more quickly.

Let's say you graduate college at twenty-two and want to buy a median-priced home by age thirty-six. That price might inflate to $550,000 by then. So, to do that, you would need to save $110,000 in fourteen years, or $7,857 a year (not counting any investment returns), to put 20 percent down.

Is that a reachable milestone? You bet. During those fourteen years, your down-payment fund can, at the least, earn a risk-free rate of return in Treasury bonds. But, given that you're so many years away from buying a home, you can afford to invest some of your down-payment funds in stocks, REITs, and other risk assets to potentially earn a greater return. In the meantime, the raises and promotions you should receive as you progress in your career will make saving up for your down payment easier. The closer you get to purchasing your home, however, the more you want to reduce risk.

Now let's say you're forty years old and want to buy a $1.5 million home in five years. You'll need to come up with $300,000 for a 20 percent down payment. Depending on your income, saving $60,000 a year won't be easy. But breaking that down into $5,000 monthly amounts can make the milestone more digestible. And, hopefully, you already have some savings, other semiliquid investments you can sell, and a decent income.

The problem most people face when buying a home is inadequate long-term planning. At twenty-two, you might be focused on finding a job you enjoy and meeting the love of your life. However, to become a millionaire, you must always think five to ten years ahead.

If you plan to purchase a home within twenty-four months, the chart below is my recommended way to invest your down payment depending on your risk tolerance. On the one hand, you'd like to invest to earn a higher return so you can buy a nicer house or take on less mortgage debt. On the other hand, you don't want to risk losing too much of your down payment; otherwise you might not be able to buy your desired home when the time comes. If you're within six months of purchasing a home, a 100 percent allocation in money market funds or Treasury bills is appropriate. For additional down payment asset allocation recommendations by time frame, please refer to my *Financial Samurai* article on how to invest your down payment.*

Recommended Asset Allocation for a Home Down Payment Fund

Buying a Home within 24 months

Risk Tolerance	Stocks	Bonds	Cash
High	50%	30%	20%
Medium	40%	30%	30%
Medium Low	20%	30%	50%
Low	0%	0%	100%

Source: FinancialSamurai.com

---

* financialsamurai.com/how-to-invest-your-down-payment-if-youre-planning-to-buy-a-house

The Importance of Owning for
Five Years or Longer

If you've found a career you enjoy and a city you want to live in for the next five years or more, it's time to start thinking about buying real estate. Ideally, when you buy a home, you believe you will live in it or own it forever. If you can't foresee yourself living in one place for at least five years, keep renting and saving the difference until you can.

The main reason why I had the courage to buy a condo in 2003 was because I had just entered business school part time at UC Berkeley. The program was three years long, and my employer paid for most of it. I wasn't going to drop out of school, and the risk of getting laid off seemed very low, so I rolled the dice and became a first-time homebuyer. I also had saved and invested 100 percent of my bonus and 50 percent of my salary for four years to come up with a $116,100 down payment.

Why is a five-year-minimum hold important? Real estate tends to move in seven-to-ten-year cycles. The longer you live in a home, the better chance you have of experiencing the upside of those cycles when you sell. Similarly, a willingness to own for a longer duration lowers your chances of having to sell on the downside of a cycle. Downturns in real estate usually range from one to five years. So, owning for at least five years can help you survive any potential recessions.

Many people don't realize there are also a lot of costs involved in selling a home—still typically between 5 percent and 6 percent of your home's value. Fortunately, costs should be decreasing in the coming years, especially after the National Association of Realtors and several brokerage houses agreed to settle a series of commission-price-fixing lawsuits in early 2024. Holding for at least five years should usually provide you with enough upside to sell at a profit despite those costs.

Busting the Real Estate Cartel

I had the privilege of hosting a fascinating discussion with attorney Mike Ketchmark on *The Financial Samurai Podcast*. You must listen to it.* In October 2023, he and his team won a landmark, $1.8 billion class action lawsuit on price fixing against the National Association of Realtors (NAR), Keller Williams, and HomeServices of America. In March 2024, in exchange for sacrificing their right to appeal, NAR agreed to pay $418 million in damages.

This was truly a David vs. Goliath moment, and it will change the real estate industry forever. Both homebuyers and home sellers should benefit from lower commissions thanks to this verdict. Instead of the standard 5 to 6 percent commission rate sellers have paid historically, commissions could easily trend down to 2 to 3 percent, on average. Just think about how it used to cost over $50 to trade a stock, but now the cost is zero online.

When I sold my first property in 2017, I couldn't believe I was paying the buyer's agent 2.5 percent while he was trying to hammer down my asking price. The buyer's agent was asking me to reduce our already agreed-upon price by $25,000 because their client wanted to change four bedroom windows due to potential leaks. Out of the 4.5 percent commission my listing agent was charging me (negotiated down from 5 percent), 2.5 percent of it was to be paid to the buyer's agent. This misaligned commission structure was jolting. The buyer

---

* financialsamurai.com/busting-real-estate-cartel-with-attorney-mike-ketchmark

should be paying their own agent, not the seller. Yet, the real estate industry argued that without paying a hefty buyer's agent commission, sellers will have a more difficult time selling their homes.

After the sale, I promised myself to not sell another property until commission rates dropped further. In addition, I ended up buying my next three properties via dual agency (with a single agent representing both the seller and buyer) to save money.* Thankfully, real estate commissions are finally coming down and are better aligned after the price-fixing verdict against NAR and other real estate brokerage firms.

If you own or are considering owning property, I urge you to listen to my episode with Ketchmark in its entirety and share it with everyone you know who is involved with buying or selling property. Given the costs and risks associated with real estate transactions, it's crucial for consumers to be fully informed about the latest changes in commissions.

If you're planning to sell a home, consider requesting a lower commission rate, which should be negotiable thanks to this significant legal case. If the potential listing agent resists, keep looking for an experienced agent who is willing to charge a lower commission. Everything is negotiable when it comes to selling and buying real estate.

For those intending to buy a home, ask your buyer's agent about the possibility of receiving a commission rebate, especially if you found the property yourself. Alternatively, ask whether the buyer's agent has a fee schedule available for you to review before signing any agreements. How buyer's agents are compensated is evolving, and it's crucial to be aware of the changes.

---

* financialsamurai.com/dual-agency

Keep the Real Estate Investing Going

One of the simplest millionaire milestone strategies for real estate is buying a primary residence, living in it for two to ten years, buying a new primary residence, and renting out the old one. This generates positive cash flow thanks to the combination of rising rents and fixed-rate mortgages. Over a forty-year period, you could potentially amass a real estate portfolio of four to twenty properties, enough to pay for your retirement forever.

Yes, it takes a lot of time and capital, but the great thing about this strategy is that you naturally grow into being a real estate investor. You're not forcing yourself to take on more debt to buy a rental property immediately. Instead, you get to enjoy a property, make improvements to it, and build more savings for your next purchase during your enjoyment period. By the time you're ready to rent out your primary residence, you should have a clear idea of its maintenance requirements. Use the 30-30-3 guidelines above and calculate 10 to 20 percent of your desired home price to determine your next target date and down payment amount. Make it a fun challenge to come up with the funds.

You win the game of real estate investing by owning the nicest house you can afford while having a portfolio of rental properties paying your living expenses. Thanks to time, leverage (taking on mortgage debt), and returns on the value of your properties, you can most certainly become a real estate millionaire with my methodology.

At Least One Rental Property for Each Member of the Family

Another real estate milestone that can keep you focused is to own one property for each member of your family plus one. If you plan to remain a lone wolf, then your goal should be to own your primary residence plus one rental property. If you have a partner but no kids, your goal should be to own your primary residence plus two rental properties. If you are married with two kids, your goal should be to own a primary residence and four rental properties, and so forth. If you only own your primary residence, you are considered neutral real estate, since you have to live somewhere. You're essentially riding the real estate wave up and down, neither getting pummeled by inflation nor benefiting from a nice current. It's only after you own more than one property that you're considered long real estate. With two or more properties, you can rent them out to take advantage of rental inflation or sell them for a potential profit.

The benefits of owning multiple properties are threefold:

1. **Generate more semi-passive retirement income.** Rents tend to go up over time, and more semi-passive income leads to more freedom.

2. **Provide career insurance for your children.** With the job market increasingly competitive, a rental property portfolio gives your children the option to manage the family properties in adulthood—that's like getting career insurance for free.

3. **The option to house each person in your family independently, if necessary.** Family life can be unpredictable. Having multiple rental properties that can be vacated if needed can provide enough housing options to ensure that nobody in your family is ever homeless and everyone is free to live their lives how they see fit. If you own rental properties near your primary residence, you also increase your chances of your children living close by as adults.

Home-to-Car Ratio

The most important personal finance ratio may be the home-to-car ratio. It's based on the notion that, while cars generally depreciate, homes tend to appreciate, making investment in housing more financially prudent than car ownership.

To calculate your home-to-car ratio, divide the estimated current value of your home by the estimated current cost of your car(s). The higher your ratio, the better, because that means your cars' value is a smaller percentage of your home's value.

The typical American has a home-to-car ratio of about 8.75 to 15.4. Your goal, if you want to attain financial freedom sooner than the masses, is a ratio above the high end of that range. Aim for a home-to-car ratio of 30 or higher. The goal is not so much to own an expensive home but to buy a more affordable car and keep it for as long as possible. Let the car's depreciation work for you, not the other way around.

The *Financial Samurai* Home-to-Car Ratio for Financial Independence

Home-to-Car Ratio	Financial Responsibility Status
< 9	You're equal to the average American or worse.
9–25	You're headed in the right direction.
25.1–50	Great progress, keep pushing.
50.1–100	Financial independence will soon be yours.
100.1–200	You're free and can do whatever the heck you want.
200+	Time to live it up, as you can't take money with you.

Home-to-Car Ratio is the value of your primary residence divided by the combined value of all your vehicles.

Source: FinancialSamurai.com

Buying too much car, especially a new car, is the most common wealth killer. With the average new-car price close to $50,000 and the median household income at about $75,000, the typical household has no business buying a new car. Yet, I've witnessed a troubling and growing trend of people purchasing expensive luxury cars alongside more modest homes or while renting, often leading to financial strain. With hefty lease payments and revolving credit card debt, many folks find themselves trapped in the rat race indefinitely.

If you do not own a primary residence yet, delay buying a car for as long as possible to save a substantial amount of money. If you do decide to buy a car, get the cheapest one you can afford and hold on to it for as long as possible. See the Further Reading section for more insights on my home-to-car ratio and my one-tenth rule for car buying.

One of the reasons I was able to buy a single-family home before I turned thirty was because I purchased a used vehicle for $8,000 and drove it for a decade. It was worth less than 3 percent of my gross annual income when I purchased it, and worth less than 1 percent of my gross annual income when I finally sold it. As a result, I was able to save a lot on car expenses and have more cash flow left over to invest in the stock market.

THE *FINANCIAL SAMURAI* WAY

To Contemplate:

☐ Only buy a property if you see yourself owning it for at least five years (preferably forever). Real estate moves in seven-to-ten-year cycles. Thinking five or more years in the future will help you minimize losses.

☐ Consider your desired car and home purchases and how cars tend to depreciate whereas homes tend to appreciate. Is your car expenditure out of whack with the value of your home? Aim for a home-to-car ratio of 30 or greater to reach financial freedom faster.

☐ Consider what your (future) grandchildren will think about property prices today.

To Do:

☐ Buy real estate as soon as you possibly can to combat inflation and allow more time for your returns to compound.

☐ Identify the median home price in the area you want to buy. Then multiply that figure by 10 to 20 percent to come up with your target down payment saving amount.

☐ To make your down-payment milestone less daunting, set a realistic time horizon and break down how much you need to save by month or year.

☐ Focus on maxing out your tax-advantaged retirement accounts first. Once your contributions are automatic, then start building your down-payment fund. Yes, you can borrow from your 401(k) penalty-free if you are a first-time homebuyer. However, it is not recommended, because you'll put your retirement at risk.

☐ Come up with a 3 to 20 percent down payment (ideally 20 percent or more) by saving aggressively with a clear target date. Consider getting assistance from the Bank of Mom and Dad, who will likely be eager to help if you show them you have thought deeply about the home purchase.

☐ Build a real estate empire one property at a time. Start by living in your primary residence for two to ten years, then rent it out and buy another. Wash, rinse, repeat.

☐ Maintain a multi-property portfolio with one property for each member of your family plus one to generate more semi-passive retirement income, provide career insurance for your children, and have the option to house each person in your family independently, if necessary.

Win Big with Entrepreneurship

THE WEALTHIEST PEOPLE ACROSS THE world are entrepreneurs. Creators of massively successful companies, such as Jeff Bezos (Amazon), Mark Zuckerberg (Meta), Larry Ellison (Oracle), Bill Gates (Microsoft), and Sergey Brin (Google), regularly top *Forbes'* list of wealthiest people.

The second wealthiest people in the world are those who invest in entrepreneurs. Investors like Warren Buffett (Berkshire Hathaway), Ken Griffin (Citadel), Abigail Johnson (Fidelity), David Tepper (Appaloosa), Steve Cohen (SAC Capital), Stephen Schwarzman (Blackstone), and Masayoshi Son (SoftBank) are all multibillionaires.

Clearly, there's something to be said about creating something from nothing and scaling a business to great fortune.

Reasons Entrepreneurship Can Launch Your Wealth

If just the thought of entrepreneurship makes you nervous, hear me out. You don't need to create a brand-new technology or a revolutionary product to be a profitable entrepreneur. Neither do you have to quit your day job cold turkey, nor devote seventy-plus hours a week, nor use your life savings to fund your own start-up. You just need to identify a problem and solve it. Then, you can leverage the internet to find people who are willing to pay for it.

To achieve great wealth, we can either invest in great entrepreneurs through the stock market or the private market, or we can create our own small businesses. But, why not do all three? You can incorporate entrepreneurship into your life by turning your existing free time toward creation instead of consumption. In addition to investing in the S&P 500, you can also allocate a small portion of your capital into private growth companies through a venture capital fund. Let's explore all of this further.

Think Small to Get Big

The problem with entrepreneurship is that people tend to fixate on the household names that have become massive empires, like Amazon or Tesla. As a result, most people think the odds of replicating that success is so low that they won't consider starting a business at all. The truth is, we don't need to create billion-dollar behemoths to become millionaires as entrepreneurs.

Every successful company started somewhere small, often no more glamorous than someone's garage, like where Google started in 1998. So, instead of being intimidated by scale, embrace thinking small as a novice entrepreneur. Don't try to come up with a wholly original idea. The simpler path is to take an existing concept and improve upon it. In the spirit of thinking small, go grab a pen and jot down three business models you feel are ripe for enhancement. Once you've envisioned the solutions, go for it. Launch! Because nothing will happen otherwise.

When I started *Financial Samurai* in 2009, there were no personal finance sites in existence that consistently published first-hand financial insights from a career finance veteran's perspective. The personal finance sites that did exist only doled out humdrum advice on saving and budgets by authors without finance backgrounds. After all, it's far easier for someone without a finance background to write about spending less than to write about asset allocation, real estate, the stock market, investing, and economic theory. Meanwhile, the real investment professionals were too busy making money from their day jobs to spend time writing for the public. I decided to fill that glaring hole in the personal finance landscape by sharing my professional wisdom, gained from earning an MBA and thirteen years of working in finance.

Looking back, this was a logical business move. Who wouldn't prefer to read in-depth personal finance articles by someone with a career in finance over posts on homeownership written by random freelancers who have only rented? Google, the largest search engine in the world, agrees. It uses the acronym E-E-A-T—Experience, Expertise, Authoritativeness, and Trustworthiness—to determine which content gets featured on its front page.

Today, *Financial Samurai*, a two-person organization composed of my wife and me, consistently generates about one million organic page views per month. This shows how much expertise matters. Our small business has led to sponsorships, book deals, speaking offers, and more. I didn't invent personal finance writing. I just made it better.

So, what frustratingly unoptimized businesses do you spot that are ripe for enhancement? (Hot tip: Whoever finally nails removable, interchangeable shoe soles will make a fortune!)

You Have the Time to Start a Business

Today, your primary income likely comes from a day job. A steady paycheck can pay for your housing, food, and basic needs, but perhaps not a whole lot more. And we all know that job security isn't what it used to be.

Unfortunately, most people rely on just *one* income stream. After work, they come home and unwind in front of the TV for three hours and doomscroll on their mobile devices for more. Stop that already.

The average millionaire has *seven* streams of income—capital gains, dividend income, interest payments, rental income, business income, royalties, and earned income. They have side businesses, passion projects, and passive income that fill and add excitement to their day-to-day lives.

If you fall into the former category, envision redirecting some of your roughly twenty-one weekly hours of TV and free time—which adds up to 1,092 hours a year—toward building something purposeful. Monetizing just one of your talents into a freelancing gig at $30 an hour could yield $32,760 in gross income a year that you could save or invest. Allocating some hours to launching your own business could generate exponentially greater earnings over time as the value of that business grows.

In the Beginning, Pay Yourself the Smallest Salary Possible

When first launching a business, pay yourself a negligible salary to minimize taxable income and maximize retained business earnings for reinvestment. As your company scales up, taking a fair market wage eventually becomes necessary to keep the IRS at bay. But for the initial two to three years, businesses aren't expected to generate that much profit.

Even CEOs of established businesses succumb to meager salaries when times are tough, and things turn out just fine for them, even great. For example, in 1978, Lee Iacocca took the role of Chrysler's CEO for a $1 salary. The company was crumbling at the time, and he thought this sacrifice would secure a government bailout and right the ship. The gambit paid off, as the company secured loans and achieved a turnaround. Iacocca's salary was $868,000 by 1980. Just six years later, his total compensation reached $20.5 million, which included a lot of stock options, landing him at the top of *Forbes'* Highest-Paid CEOs list.

The dollar-a-year salvo is practically a rite of passage now for executives navigating corporate hardship. Steve Jobs, James Barksdale, John Chambers, Thomas Siebel, Larry Ellison—all icons of tech—also took $1 salaries to signal they were highly committed to the survival of their companies.

But how can you survive earning practically nothing? *The best way is to build your business while you're still employed.* With your preexisting W-2 job providing steady income and benefits, you can focus on thoughtful growth on the side rather than scrambling to make quick cash just to survive.

I followed this model when I started *Financial Samurai*. I was still working in finance and ran the site as a personal journal, written during nonwork hours. To avoid conflicts, I never publicized any perspectives that could impact my employment. Instead, I just published my own thoughts on topics such as buying an investment property or surviving the financial crisis.

I didn't even incorporate my business until after I negotiated a severance in 2012 and left Wall Street to focus on growing the site more intently. Those initial years incubating the site part time provided an invaluable foundation for its sixteen-plus years of ongoing operation.

Equity Is What Will Make You Rich, Not Your Salary

When it comes to running a business, it is the equity you own in that business, not your salary, that will help make you a millionaire or multimillionaire. To increase your business's chances of surviving during its initial years, keep your expenses as low as possible.

The magic of owning equity is that it increases in value by a multiple set by the market. When you make a $50,000 salary, that's all you get. But, as an owner, if businesses in your industry trade at a rate of five times earnings, and you increase your business's net profit by $50,000, you would have increased the value of your equity by five times that net profit, or $250,000. The growth in your equity is the true wealth-building power of running a business.

Investors determine valuation based on multiples of metrics such as earnings, revenue, and operating profit. The price-to-earnings (P/E) ratio is most common—it represents how much investors are willing to pay per dollar of a business's annual earnings. For example, if a semiconductor chipmaker earns $10 a share and trades at $200 per share, it has a P/E of twenty (200/10). That means the market is valuing the company at twenty times its annual earnings. If that company has $100 million in annual earnings, the market will value it at $2 billion.

Let's say that same company announces it has a breakthrough in semiconductor design and will be launching the fastest-ever chip to power artificial intelligence. The company's share price rockets to $400 per share in anticipation of increased earnings. It is now trading on a P/E of forty (400/10) because the share price has gone up but its earnings per share has yet to change. Suddenly, the company is valued at $4 billion, based on forty times its current net profit of $100 million, mainly because of market expectations for greater future earnings. If the company's earnings per share eventually doubles to $20 and the company's share price remains at $400, its P/E multiple will revert back to twenty. In other words, a large part of investing in risk assets, like stocks, is based on the company's—or its assets'—future earnings potential. If earnings surpass current market estimates, the stock will likely appreciate in value. If earnings fall short of expectations, the opposite will likely occur.

The key takeaway here is that every marginal dollar earned through your business gets multiplied into outsized valuation gains. Meanwhile, the larger the percentage of the business you own, the more value you get to capture. Let's say you own 100 percent of a business that generates $100,000 a year in net profit. If it's in an industry where companies trade at ten times earnings, congratulations! You now own a $1 million business. Every dollar in profit increases the value of your business by $10.

In terms of becoming a millionaire through entrepreneurship, the possibilities are greater than you think. Think small by solving a specific problem and work your way up. As you gain experience and expertise, you will be able to identify new business opportunities over time.

Think Like an Investor to Understand the Power of Entrepreneurship

Imagine discovering a company that reliably generates $1 million in profits year after year. As an investor, you'd race to buy it for only $1 million if you could, because the payback period would only be one year. Plus, every subsequent year could deliver income straight into your pocket.

Now picture yourself as that business's owner. Would you sell something that can produce an endless stream of wealth for a measly P/E of one? No, you'd realize your baby's potential as a forever enterprise and would demand a king's ransom for it. As the owner of a business, as opposed to a mere employee, you also have the option of a liquidity jackpot by selling your business in the future.

And that, my aspiring entrepreneur, is the mindset that has driven countless entrepreneurs before you. Sweat and sacrifice fuel something greater than yourself—a legacy poised to continuously generate income and leave a long-lasting impact. Now that you know the massive potential of entrepreneurship, how will you spend this day? The choice is yours.

A Business Fork in the Road

A month before I permanently left my job in finance in May of 2012, I had a dilemma. I was wondering whether I should strive to grow a comfortable lifestyle business or create a big, venture-backed company with a potentially enormous payout. Living in San Francisco in the early 2000s, I couldn't help but be bombarded with dreams of a mega-million- or even billion-dollar start-up.

That year, *Financial Samurai* was on pace to generate about $80,000, enough to provide a simple life for my wife and me in our expensive city. As frugal people, $80,000 was enough. However, it wouldn't be enough if our family grew to include a couple of children. Should I think bigger?

A Night at the Poker Table

One night, back in 2012, the fellas and I were playing poker and got to talking about what we always talked about: entrepreneurship. I loved going to Friday night poker, mainly because I got to bounce ideas off really smart people.

Out of a table of ten, four worked at start-ups, three were at Google, one was a high-tech lawyer, another worked as a medical correspondent for CNN, and then there was me, a hybrid.

Before I arrived, I had spent three hours writing on *Financial Samurai* after working a ten-hour day in finance. Needless to say, I was a little tired.

When I heard stories of how one start-up poker player was working from seven a.m. to three a.m. the next morning every day for two weeks straight to launch a product offering, I got pumped. When the venture capitalist poker player recounted how his firm rejected a pitch by Tim Westergren, Pandora's founder, in 2008, I winced but daydreamed in amazement.

Down about $185 for the evening, I started lamenting about how long I would have to work at my side hustle to earn back the money I lost. Several hours at least, I thought. How depressing, all thanks to my opponent's king on the river crushing my pocket queens.

Not one to dwell in the doldrums, I quickly shifted to more pleasant thoughts about the future of start-ups.

The Comfortable Lifestyle Business or the Big Payout?

I posed this question in between hands to my fellow sharks:

> Would you rather make $10,000 a month for the rest of your life indexed to inflation and only have to work two to four hours a day, or make minimum wage working twelve to eighteen hours a day for two years with a 25 percent chance of selling your business for $10 million? If the business doesn't succeed, all you'll be left with are your experiences.

I purposefully left the question open-ended to see what their various responses would be. Already, I could see one was doing math equations on what the capitalized value of $10,000 a month would be based on an average life expectancy compared to the expected value of the big payout. After all, we calculate expected value all the time in poker.

I encouraged my fellow players to stop calculating and go with their gut. Surely, at least half would choose the handsome sum of $10,000 a month and live happily ever after, given it was roughly two times the median household income in America. Surprisingly, every single one of them chose option two: the potential big payout, which I found somewhat delusional, but it's always nice to dream big.

As the night wore on, I finally heard someone take the lifestyle entrepreneur side after losing $690 in a $2,600, four-way pot when his straight got flushed out.

He muttered, "Well, $10,000 a month for working only a couple hours a day isn't so bad. I think I'll go with that."

A Lifestyle Business Can Be Wonderful

More than a decade has passed since that memorable poker night full of lofty, entrepreneurial dreams. While no one at the table has yet to cash in on those $10 million visions, the lessons remain. Attempting to build big requires courage. That shouldn't be discounted. Even if great fortune doesn't favor the bold, the personal growth and satisfaction from going all in on your own idea is immense.

Lifestyle businesses harbor their own underrated value. The venture-capitalist and start-up crowd may mock modest entrepreneurial pursuits. However, optimized freedom, flexibility, and purpose-aligned work can generate plenty of rewards for those who are uninterested in traditional scaling.

Just look at *Financial Samurai*, a humble site born without funding rounds or exit strategies. This lifestyle business still enables me and my wife, its sole founders, to be stay-at-home parents to two kids in expensive San Francisco. Though my net worth may not yet rival those who can afford to purchase vacation properties in Aspen, this path has unlocked the wealth that matters most to me: time.

Wealth can come in many forms, including money, status, freedom, health, and spirituality. Once you pass forty, you might find that freedom, health, and spirituality are by far the most important types of wealth to obtain.

The 3-30-3 Framework for Entrepreneurship

I understand that becoming an entrepreneur can be daunting. What if you start a business and lose all your money? You might face financial and social shame as your risk-averse peers whisper behind your back.

To maximize your chances of success, follow my 3-30-3 entrepreneurship framework. Work on your business for three years while keeping the security of a W-2 paycheck. Grow your business's net profit to cover at least 30 percent of your living expenses. Then, take a leap of faith and go all in on your business for three years. If it doesn't work out, you can always return to your old job for similar pay.

You don't have to follow my 3-30-3 framework exactly if you need more time or your business's profits are growing faster than expected. The key is to be intentional every step of the way. At some point, spending forty-plus hours a week at your day job will hold your business back. On the other hand, if your business has stalled after three years, it's probably time to return to work to avoid draining your funds.

If Entrepreneurship Isn't for You

Not everyone desires or can manage entrepreneurship. That's perfectly all right. You can take a simpler route by investing in great, established businesses. For most people, low-cost index funds tracking the S&P 500 hit the optimal balance of diversification, responsibility, and efficiency. Investing in the S&P 500 index should be your main public equity investment. However, these five hundred companies are typically multibillion-dollar giants that aren't very entrepreneurial anymore, just operational and focused on taking incremental market share.

If you truly want to invest in entrepreneurs, consider venture capital (VC), which is riskier and illiquid but offers tremendous upside if you can find the next unicorn. If you invest in a fund that invests in the next Apple, your returns will be incredible. But accessing top-tier VC funds that have first looks at the best private companies can be challenging.

As an alternative, consider open-ended evergreen funds that offer ongoing flexibility, no lock-up periods, and transparency in evaluating their holdings before committing capital. Some open-ended venture funds have investment minimums as low as $10 and charge lower fees as well.* There are a growing number of open-ended venture capital funds to choose from.

Investing in private companies carries significantly more risk than investing in public companies with established businesses. A common understanding is that roughly one out of every ten venture-funded businesses succeeds in providing a positive return to shareholders. However, drawing from my experience as a venture capital investor for more than twenty years and a lifestyle business owner for more than sixteen, the rewards are worth a portion of your capital.

---

* Learn more at financialsamurai.com/innovation.

Unless you possess expertise in evaluating private companies, I do not recommend investing directly into individual ventures as an angel investor. Without a distinct advantage, your chances of success are limited. Instead, consider investing in top-tier venture funds, allocating up to 20 percent of your investable assets. The associated fees are high (ranging from 1 percent to 2 percent of assets under management, plus 20 percent to 35 percent of profits), but they are the cost of accessing promising opportunities and potentially high returns. Companies are staying private for longer, meaning more of their gains are being accrued to private investors. It's prudent to asset allocate accordingly.

The Entrepreneurial Mindset for Success

Whether you are embarking on your entrepreneurial journey or supporting ventures as an investor, cultivating an entrepreneurial mindset is paramount to becoming a millionaire. Discard the notion that traditional routes, such as a nine-to-five job coupled with diligent saving and investing, are the sole paths to amassing wealth.

Challenge yourself to perpetually explore avenues for scaling your products or honing your skills and aim for greater rewards. Entrepreneurs distinguish themselves by contemplating the future, ceaselessly striving to innovate or enhance existing processes. They defy the status quo, unraveling solutions where others perceive insurmountable problems. You'd be surprised by how much will come to you if you sit quietly in a hot tub for an hour.

Resilience is a hallmark of entrepreneurs. They endure setbacks and failures, recognizing that these are integral facets of any journey. Triumph arises from learning, and entrepreneurs embrace setbacks as steppingstones toward eventual success. View your failures as teachable moments, and your happiness and overall success will increase.

Lifelong learning is another key ingredient for entrepreneurial success. Engaging with industry trends, seeking new knowledge, and remaining receptive to constructive feedback exemplify the commitment successful entrepreneurs exhibit. School doesn't end after high school or college. Learning is forever.

Lastly, successful entrepreneurs are resolute in action. Rejecting hazardous overthinking, they make decisions and propel themselves toward their objectives. When things don't go according to plan, they pivot. Their indispensable ability to execute translates ideas into reality. Nothing will ever get done if you don't act.

Whether charting your course as an entrepreneur or supporting others on their journey, embracing the entrepreneurial mindset can be transformative. Get ready to propel yourself toward unprecedented achievements.

THE *FINANCIAL SAMURAI* WAY

To Contemplate:

☐ Think small to get big. To get any business idea off the ground, limit your initial scope to increase your likelihood of launching.

☐ Adopt the entrepreneurial mindset in everything you do. Contemplate the future, look for ways to innovate and scale, and commit to lifelong learning. Be resilient, decisive, and act.

☐ Understand the power of leverage when you own a business. Your business is valued at a multiple of revenue or profits. Every dollar your business brings in increases your business's value by much more.

☐ If you don't want to start a business, you can invest in those who do via venture funds. Open-ended VC funds are an easy entry point due to flexibility, transparency, and low investment minimums.

To Do:

☐ Write down three business models you feel are ripe for enhancement. Pick one that you want to tackle. Then put together a business plan and launch. Forming an S corporation or LLC is not necessary in the beginning.

☐ To increase your chances of entrepreneurial success, follow my 3-30-3 framework. It says to work on your business for three years on the side while having a day job to grow your company enough to cover 30 percent or more of your living expenses. Then dedicate three years of your life to your business full time before deciding what's next.

☐ When first launching a business, pay yourself a negligible salary and minimize expenses to increase your chances of survival. Ideally, start it on the side while you're still employed. Steady pay and job benefits reduce profit pressure and buy runway. Remember, equity is what will make you rich, not your salary.

☐ Count your income streams. Identify which types you're missing from the millionaire seven. Then list out the ones you're missing and create a milestone to dive into each of them this year.

Lifestyle—The Millionaire Way of Life

THERE'S NOT MUCH POINT IN WORKING SO HARD ON milestones to grow your wealth only to blow yourself up and your money alongside you. But in reality, we all make countless mistakes in life, especially when it comes to money, me included.

In this section, we'll go over all types of goof-ups and bad decisions others have made so you don't have to do the same. Then, we'll dip into some recent insights on why your location has a direct impact on your wealth trajectory even in this day and age of remote work. Lastly, we'll round off the section by intertwining money, marriage, and family to show how you can use milestones to lead a well-balanced, harmonious, and prosperous lifestyle.

Evade Financial Land Mines and Conquer the Unexpected

WHENEVER THERE'S A TASK THAT requires effort and diligence, people will come up with a list of excuses as to why they couldn't get it done. Saving money is no different.

Fortunately, you now have this book and aren't going to let yourself down any longer. You *will* save each month. And even small, incremental increases *will* make a difference in your quest to become a millionaire.

What's next? Making sure you don't step on a land mine along the way.

Dodging Money Mistakes

It might seem obvious that it's to your benefit to steer clear of making grave errors with your money. But many of us are inherently stubborn, think we're immune to financial disasters, or believe we're smarter than we actually are. For example, a retired law enforcement officer, who thought he, of all people, had the ability to sniff out untrustworthy people, wound up losing more than $900,000 in a time-share scam run by a Mexican drug cartel.

Meanwhile, every day, retail investors buy and sell individual stocks believing they can outperform the stock market in the long run. Overwhelming data suggests that they cannot. Even professional investors struggle to do so. Then, one day, the retail investor faces a 50 percent loss on a stock, meaning they now need a 100 percent gain just to break even. Yet, they sell and continue a cycle of poorly timed trades with inappropriate risk exposure. Regrettably, financial mishaps like this, along with numerous others in various degrees and formats, occur frequently.

It's crucial not only to ensure you don't fall victim to scams but also to safeguard your assets from self-inflicted wounds. Keep your FOMO and desires in check, as such emotions can derail the financial progress of even the savviest individuals. Stay vigilant about your financial health, as it's easy to let things slide over time. Acknowledge where your knowledge and expertise are lacking and strive for continuous self-improvement. Neglecting these factors may lead you to lament *Why me?* in a puddle of self-pity on the sofa one day.

Common Financial Setbacks to Avoid

I want to highlight some costly mistakes to help you make better financial choices on your journey toward millionaire milestones. Having this knowledge can save you time and reduce anxiety by safeguarding your wealth-building goals from potential derailment due to errors or poor decision-making. I'll cover relationship land mines, including the costs of divorce, in Milestone 10.

Neglecting Your Credit

Many large banking institutions, such as Citi and Chase, offer customers easy access to monitor their credit scores. Check with your personal banker for details. If you are not already monitoring your credit score regularly, it's time to make it a priority.

Why? Low credit scores can impact your financial health in many ways. It can be harder to get loans. You may have to pay high interest rates on borrowed debt. You may have to pay more for insurance and rent.

In case you're unfamiliar with the scoring system or need a refresher, FICO scores are based on the following numeric ranges.

800–900 = Exceptional

740–799 = Very Good

670–739 = Good

580–669 = Fair

250–579 = Risky

Scores are composed of five different elements. Payment history accounts for 35 percent. Your debt influences 30 percent. The length of your credit history impacts 15 percent. Any new credit opened affects 10 percent. And the types of credit you have determine the remaining 10 percent.

Set a goal to achieve and maintain an exceptional credit score. Stay organized. Make all your payments on time. Don't borrow too much. Keep the frequency with which you apply for credit low. Build your credit history. Keep your credit utilization (your outstanding credit card balance divided by the combined credit limits of your credit cards) below 25 percent.

A great credit score not only provides you easier access to credit, it also enables you to borrow at a lower rate. A lower interest rate could make the difference between affording a home at a great price and getting priced out.

Believe it or not, another benefit to having a high credit score is making you look more appealing as a person. With your written permission, some employers may ask to screen your credit before making a hiring decision. There are even dating apps that require a minimum credit score of 675 to be on the platform.

Succumbing to Greed

Whatever your circumstances are, be careful not to waste your hard-earned money on needless things. Poor debt management with revolving, high-interest balances, such as credit card debt, payday loans, and personal loans, not only prevents you from growing wealth, it can cause your finances to go in reverse.

Overspending and the inability to make your savings last are a recipe for financial ruin. Not even the great Warren Buffett, who is worth more than $100 billion, has been able to secure a compound annual return greater than the average credit card interest rate.

Psychologically, you must overcome the belief that you deserve what you have not yet earned. Otherwise, you will have a very difficult—if not impossible—time achieving the millionaire milestones in this book.

I hope you achieve more wealth in your lifetime than you ever imagined. But please have the humility of knowing that greed could literally wipe it all away. No fortune, however vast, is immune from greed or poor decisions. Staying grounded and vigilant, even at the highest peaks of wealth, remains paramount. Being satisfied with enough is one of the keys to wealth.

Inaccurately Extrapolating Your Income

Use caution when projecting your income many years into the future. The higher your income, the more volatile it is likely to be. For example, top earners in investment banking can make $1 million or more a year, but once you reach that level of compensation, it doesn't continually go up and to the right. In fact, given that much of their total compensation is composed of discretionary year-end bonuses, total compensation can easily drop by 70 percent or more during downturns.

High incomes tend to spike and drop because they are typically performance correlated, market driven, under more scrutiny, and at the mercy of many factors out of the employees' control. Lower incomes tend to be more stable.

An Unexpected Outcome

In 2007, I felt like I just couldn't lose. As a third-year vice president at Credit Suisse, I was earning the highest income I had ever made. Instead of saving, I opted to buy a two-bedroom vacation condo in Palisades Tahoe for $720,000.

At the time, I thought it was a good deal, as the seller had bought it for $815,000 just a year earlier. Unfortunately, the condo's value plummeted by 50 percent during the global financial crisis, leaving me regretful for purchasing something I didn't truly need.

I had assumed that my income would continue to rise over the next five to ten years. However, in 2008, my income dropped by 40 percent. Over the remainder of my finance career, I never reached the same level of financial success as I had in 2007.

> Before you purchase a big-ticket item, plan out optimistic, realistic, and pessimistic scenarios about your income and wealth. If you cannot afford to purchase that item and maintain it in a pessimistic scenario, don't buy it.

Underestimating Your Expenses and Tax Liabilities

When you are planning for your future and eventual retirement, having a realistic estimate of your expenses and tax liabilities is crucial. Use helpful, free retirement calculator tools available on the internet to get a better handle on your finances.* The more you can track your finances, the better you can optimize.

Yes, it's impossible to know the future and predict exactly how much you will need and spend down the road. But it's important to get as close to it as possible and be prepared to adjust your spending to how much you ultimately have at your disposal.

One year, I decided to pay myself a $160,000 salary from my S corp business, up from $120,000 the year prior. I was confident about the future and didn't mind paying a 24 percent marginal federal income tax rate. However, I failed to anticipate that I would receive a large capital distribution from a private real estate fund investment I had made many years prior. That pushed me up into the 32 percent income tax bracket. As a result, I ended up paying about $25,000 more in taxes that year than I expected, all because of suboptimal income and tax planning.

---

* financialsamurai.com/free-wealth-management

Going All In on Margin

In your quest to achieve $1 million, you may be tempted to go super aggressive on your investments. One such method is trading on margin. For the vast majority of people, this is a suboptimal investment strategy, because attempting to outperform the market is a fool's errand long term.

If you're unfamiliar with it, trading on margin simply means taking out a loan with a broker-dealer to execute trades, a method distinct from trading via traditional cash accounts. There are several reasons why this is a bad idea.

First, it transforms you into an active investor who is trying to time the market. Such an approach is known for falling short of passive index investments over the long term. Even the majority of professionals underperform over periods of five and ten years. It is thus an even more risky endeavor for the average person. Additionally, by utilizing margin to purchase stocks, you are accumulating debt to fund your investments, thus magnifying their underperformance. If you're not careful, all of your equity could get wiped out.

Moreover, the borrowing costs associated with margin trading are significant, ranging from 4 percent up to 14 percent, on average. This expense primarily benefits brokers or brokerage firms, which earn interest on your margin debt.

The emotional toll is another drawback. With gains and losses heightened, investors can turn into tempestuous wrecks on volatile days. This emotional turbulence can negatively impact your relationships with your partner and children.

Furthermore, you might be forced to sell your position at the worst time if your stocks tank as margin calls come due (a margin call is a demand from a brokerage firm to increase the amount of equity in your account when it dips below their required minimum). Losing lots of money buying stocks on margin means you are also losing valuable time. Having to work one, three, five, or even ten more years to make up for your losses would be atrocious and negatively affect other aspects of your life.

Although margin trading can serve specific, short-term purposes, such as expediting fund transfers, its overall drawbacks make it an unwise choice for long-term investments.

Day Trading

Day trading is a waste of time and money. The return on effort will be pitiful, and you will get stressed out. You are much better off investing in long-term trends and dominant companies that are consistently growing their earnings and dividends. Let C-level executives and their employees do the work for you. Day trading is the exact opposite of buy-and-hold investing, because you're continuously putting in effort to seek out a return.

I first started day trading my junior year of college and continued all throughout my twenties while working on Wall Street. It proved to be a career-limiting move because day trading was a distraction and exhausting. It's no wonder my manager pulled me aside a couple of times to tell me to tone things down. Once I hit my thirties, I rarely day traded, because I realized I could make much more money if I focused on my career.

Over the long term, trying to time the market doesn't work. Most likely, all you'll be left with is a massive number of trades to reconcile come tax time, with only meager profits, if you're lucky. If you hold stocks for less than a year, you'll have to pay higher, short-term capital gains taxes on any profits, further reducing returns.

Don't day trade if you care about what's good for you.

Mismanaging Your Investments' Risk Profile

Understanding and managing your risk tolerance in investing is crucial for long-term success.

People consistently overestimate how much money they are willing to lose, because they've never really gone through a serious bear market, like the one we experienced in 2008. If you take too much risk, you might wipe away all the gains that took you a lifetime to earn. If you take too little risk, you might not reach your financial goals in the time frame you want.

To quantify your risk tolerance, I suggest asking yourself how much time you're willing to give up in order to make up for potential investment losses. The more extra time you're willing to work to make up for your losses, the higher your risk tolerance, and vice versa. This is my Samurai Equity Exposure Rule (SEER).

I use a simple formula to quantify risk tolerance:

$$\frac{Public\ Equity\ Exposure \times 35\%}{Monthly\ Gross\ Income} = Risk\ Tolerance$$

The 35 percent comes from the average drawdown of stocks in a bear market. For example, if you have $500,000 in equities and you earn $10,000 a month, your risk tolerance is equal to 500,000 × 35% / 10,000. That works out to 175,000 / 10,000, or 17.5. That means you will need to work seventeen and a half *additional* months of your life, nearly a year and a half, to earn a *gross* income equal to how much you lost in a –35 percent bear market. After taxes, you're likely only making around $8,000 a month, so you will actually have to work closer to twenty-two more months and contribute 100 percent of your after-tax income from that period to be whole.

A moderate risk tolerance corresponds to a willingness to work between twelve and twenty-four months to recoup your investment losses. A high risk tolerance means being willing to work for more than thirty-six months, or three years, to make back your losses. Personally, as a tired forty-seven-year-old dad of two young children, I'm unwilling to work more than twelve months to make up for my losses. Therefore, I consider myself a moderate-to-conservative investor. You have to decide how much time you're willing to sacrifice to make up for potential losses.

We do not know what we do not know. Therefore, it's important to run through different scenarios when it comes to investing and planning for your retirement. With regards to return assumptions, I put my 401(k) and taxable investments through three different scenarios—Conservative, Realistic, and Blue-Sky*—to see whether there will be enough for me to live on by the time I'm in my sixties. Instead of modeling out your returns on a spreadsheet, you can use any number of free online retirement calculators to get your results quicker.

Managing your risk tolerance is always going to be important. Therefore, you should do a deep-dive analysis of your holdings each year. After every down year, have a heart-to-heart discussion with a loved one or trusted friend about your investment decisions and how they made you feel. Discuss what went wrong and how you might have done things differently if you could rewind time. Discovering your true risk tolerance takes recurrent fine-tuning over the years.

Lending Money

There's a difference between spotting a friend $30 at a cash-only bar and lending out anything more than $100 for whatever purpose. When someone asks to borrow more than the cost of one meal or a couple drinks, things can get awkward. If you decline,

---

* financialsamurai.com/how-to-better-manage-your-401k-for-retirement-through-sce nario-analysis

you may damage your relationship. If you say yes, your relationship could still disintegrate if they don't pay you back on time, or at all, which could breed deep resentment.

A better approach is to refrain from lending money altogether. If someone close to you is in dire need of money, and you have ample means, consider making it a gift instead. You can decide whether or not to disclose to the recipient that it's a gift, but the key is to have no expectation of getting paid back. If your friend does get back on their feet financially and repays your kindness, it will feel like a bonus.

Navigate Your Way Past Unexpected Variables

One lesson I continually teach the *Financial Samurai* community is to account for unexpected variables. Even if you have the best plans in the world, life doesn't move in a straight line. There will be delays, bumps, twists, potholes, turns, detours, and even giant sinkholes along the way. Even though you will be better prepared for financial success after reading this book, you may experience a monetary setback after a layoff, divorce, unfortunate medical issue, suboptimal decision, or any number of other unforeseen circumstances. Sometimes we can do everything right and still get financially screwed.

Perhaps you've heard the expression *hope for the best, expect the worst*. The better you are at *expecting the unexpected*, the higher your chances of long-term success. Premortem planning—having contingency plans in place *before* something goes wrong—takes extra thought and effort, but it can greatly improve your ability to navigate life's surprises.

What Are the Chances?!

At my son's school, there's an attendance monitor who marks children late as soon as the clock strikes 8:30 a.m. After six late arrivals, the teachers speak to the parents about the student's tardiness.

I strive to ensure we always arrive at school five minutes early. But, one morning, we faced an unexpected obstacle on our commute: a massive eucalyptus tree had fallen into the street, blocking three out of four lanes. A heavy rainstorm the previous night had saturated the soil, causing numerous downed trees. On top of that, the traffic lights were out. Things got even worse when a car up ahead T-boned another car.

We were fifteen minutes late due to poor planning and that multitude of unexpected variables. Now, whenever it storms, we leave earlier for school the next morning so we have a larger buffer to avoid arriving late.

There's an old Yiddish saying, *Mensch tracht, un Gott lacht*, which means "Man plans, and God laughs." Whatever can go wrong will go wrong in life. Always plan for adverse scenarios.

Changing Careers Won't Solve All Your Money Issues

How many times have you vented about how much you hate your job and wished you were *doing something else*? Probably a lot. Studies show most employees are disengaged from work. Unfortunately, change is hard, and changing careers to a new industry can slow down your trek to becoming a millionaire, especially if you haven't reached the $250,000 crossover point yet. If you really want to head down a new path, make sure you research the risks thoroughly before taking that leap. A lot of time and money is at stake.

From a financial perspective, map out all the costs associated with changing careers. For example, if you want to go to business school full time for two years, add up the total costs of business school, the forgone salary, and the lost time. Then compare that total to your potential income and increased happiness in your new career.

If you plan to transition to a new career, you'll likely have to take a step down in pay. Try to sit down with a veteran in the field you want to join to gain insights on all the pros and cons. It is very common to experience disappointment after a career change if you don't have proper expectations.

If you decide to leave a job you no longer enjoy, I recommend negotiating a severance instead of quitting. If you're successful, you could not only get a severance check but also subsidized health care, deferred compensation, and unemployment benefits. Having a financial runway is a huge advantage during a career-transition period. My ebook *How to Engineer Your Layoff** is the perfect resource to help you with severance negotiations.

Shield Yourself from Bankruptcy

We've all lost money in our lives, some significantly more than others. Nobody ever wants to fail, but you can crawl out of even the deepest hole with the right tools and enough resolve. Even some of the most successful people make bad investments, lose track of their spending, and go broke. The smartest and most determined of them own up to and learn from their mistakes. They lean in to their talents and connections to come back stronger than ever.

---

* financialsamurai.com/how-to-make-money-quitting-your-job-2

For example, if there's any renowned pop star who is fearless about self-expression, relentlessly devoted to fine-tuning her craft, and not afraid to shock the world, it's Lady Gaga. But did you know she went bankrupt amid her rising fame? After her second worldwide concert tour, The Monster Ball, she was $3 million in debt despite her growing stardom. That tour was extremely successful from a promotional standpoint, but the number of changes she wanted to the show made it one of the least profitable. What's fascinating is that she didn't even know she was that deep in debt until other people started talking about her being broke.

Fortunately, Lady Gaga went on to have many more hit singles, albums, and tours. She also appeared in multiple TV shows and films, winning an Oscar for her original song "Shallow" from the movie *A Star Is Born*, which she starred in opposite Bradley Cooper. Roughly thirteen years after she was $3 million in debt, her net worth skyrocketed to roughly $150 million.

Although some people have great comeback stories after bad financial decisions, many others do not. Practice prudence with your finances. The game is never really over when it comes to personal finance, and there's no automatic restart. If you get wiped out, you will need the mental strength to pull yourself back up and get back to work to slowly recover your losses.

Protect Yourself from Big Losses

Losing small amounts of money here and there is fine. The big losses are what you want to avoid along your millionaire journey.

Navigating financial pitfalls and overcoming unexpected challenges demands strategic planning and a solid defense. But here's the kicker: It's not only about warding off external threats. It's equally crucial to shield yourself from your own occasional missteps and hasty decisions.

Find that sweet spot of equilibrium by placing a premium on your health, happiness, and success. Master that, and you're not just in the clear, you're on the path to millions.

THE *FINANCIAL SAMURAI* WAY

To Contemplate:

☐ Consider *why* you and those closest to you have made excuses about money in terms of splurging recklessly, not saving for retirement, mismanaging time, avoiding hard tasks, and/or lacking motivation or knowledge. Now imagine how great things could be with proper action.

☐ Be careful not to inaccurately extrapolate your income, expenses, or taxes. The higher your income, the more volatile it is likely to be in the future.

To Do:

☐ Stop making excuses. Start saving, and make it as automatic as possible. Remember, you're gunning for the $250,000 benchmark.

☐ Run through a list of things you are thankful for on a weekly basis to avoid succumbing to greed, overspending, and FOMO.

☐ Protect your credit like it's your own baby. Make payments on time, don't borrow too much, build your credit history, and keep your credit utilization below 25 percent. Set a milestone to achieve and maintain an exceptional credit score (800-plus).

☐ Come up with your own investment framework and manage it continually. Quantify your risk tolerance by using my SEER formula every six months.

- ☐ Don't lend money to friends and family. If you genuinely want to help someone and are able, consider a monetary gift instead of a loan.

- ☐ Avoid going all in on margin, and don't waste time and money day trading, because you won't be able to outperform the market long term.

- ☐ Carefully calculate the costs of changing careers and avoid making any sudden moves.

- ☐ Stay humble and protected. The more you can plan for unexpected variables and hardships, the more you can shield your finances from large losses.

Be Where the Money Is

IF YOU WANT TO GET, and stay, rich, being in the right place at the right time is more important than you think. There are two components to this phrase: the "right place" and the "right time." Being in the right place is easier to control. And, if you move to the right city, then your chances of good timing increase. You could be the smartest, hardest-working, best-looking, most charismatic person ever, but you are unlikely to get rich if the largest employer in your town is a greasy spoon restaurant.

I'll always remember getting the best darn grilled cheese sandwich ever in Abingdon, Virginia, where my girlfriend's parents lived at the time. Abingdon was a five-hour drive from Williamsburg, Virginia, where we were attending the College of William & Mary. Abingdon was a beautiful town with some friendly people. But, after eating at the diner, there was nothing else to do except wander around Roses Discount Store and look up at the stars after dark. When my girlfriend's father found a KKK flyer in his mailbox the day after I arrived, I decided that, as an Asian American, maybe Abingdon wasn't a place I should settle down and grow my fortune.

Reasons to Live in a High-Income Metropolis

One of the best ways to increase your chances of making more money is to move to a city that has a lot of high-paying jobs. Ideally, you'll secure an offer before moving to one of these cities. Otherwise, when you first arrive, you may have to suck it up and share a room in the cheapest place you can find.

There's no denying that the work-from-home movement enabled many people to relocate to more affordable areas within their city or even around the country. However, not all industries and firms support working from home to the same degree, if at all, anymore. Plus, working from home is best reserved for after you've already established a solid footing in your career with several promotions under your belt. Otherwise, you risk hampering your growth potential by being out of physical sight and absent from the office's social environment.

High-income metro areas can not only benefit your career and earning prospects through higher salaries, greater networking opportunities, and access to innovative technologies and start-ups, but they can also improve your lifestyle. Top metro areas offer easy access to top-tier education, vibrant culture and entertainment, premium medical facilities and health-care specialists, diversity, well-developed infrastructure, better services, more investment opportunities, and higher property resale values.

Whether you relocate to a current top-income area or not, do consider investing in real estate in one, as winners tend to keep on winning. Revisit Milestone 6 for a refresher on the importance of real estate to growing wealth.

Metropolitan Areas with Top Incomes

Where in the US have people been making the most money? Let's look at some data from the US Department of Commerce in 2023 on the top ten metropolitan areas with the highest incomes. Six of the ten—those shaded in the following table—had strong staying power and have ranked in the top ten for two decades or more. One could say those cities were able to build upon their positive network effects.

Metropolitan Area Rankings by Income

	1980 Rank	2021 Rank
San Jose-Sunnyvale-Santa Clara, CA	4	1
Bridgeport-Stamford-Norwalk, CT	1	2
San Francisco-Oakland-Berkeley, CA	3	3
Boston-Cambridge-Newton, MA/NH	31	4
Seattle-Tacoma-Bellevue, WA	8	5
Washington-Arlington-Alexandria, DC/VA/MD/WV	2	6
New York-Newark-Jersey City, NY/NJ/PA	14	7
Denver-Aurora-Lakewood, CO	7	8
Austin-Round Rock-Georgetown, TX	55	9
Fayetteville-Springdale-Rogers, AR	107	10

Per-capita income ranking out of 110 largest US metro areas with a 2020 population of 500,000 or more people

Sources: US Department of Commerce, US Bureau of Economic Analysis

Unexpected Arkansas

For those of you who aren't familiar with the tenth-ranked area in that table, Fayetteville–Springdale–Rogers, Arkansas, this metropolitan area is located in the Ozarks near the city of

Bentonville. Sam and Helen Walton, of Walmart fame, moved here in their early thirties and their company's headquarters remains there today. Two other *Fortune* 500 companies, Tyson Foods and J. B. Hunt, are also headquartered in the area.

Northwest Arkansas features many outdoor activities and music festivals that appeal to a young, hip crowd and is one of the bicycling meccas of America. The entire state of Arkansas boasts some of the most beautiful camping, hiking, and fishing spots in the country. Meanwhile, according to Zillow, the median home price in Little Rock, the most expensive city in Arkansas, is only about $210,000, less than half the median home price in America.

The highest-income areas truly have a lot to offer in a variety of environments, from bustling cities on either coast to cities in the serene mountains. However, if you're looking to live near the beach in Honolulu, you'll have to wait to move there until after you've made your millions. Not only is Honolulu one of the most expensive cities to live in, the average pay is lower than on the mainland, even in similar jobs.

I'm biased toward San Francisco, since I've lived there since 2001. It's the metropolitan area many people—including the media—love to hate given its weather, high cost of living, politics, and tremendous wealth creation over the years. It may be expensive to live in the Bay Area, but the opportunities to make large sums of money are ubiquitous.

Before San Francisco, I lived in New York City, the best city in the world, for *six* months a year due to harsh weather during the other months. Although I had to share a studio apartment for a couple of years, I had a blast. As a poor, recent college graduate, I had to learn how to save money and make my income go further. If you end up in one of these expensive cities, you will too.

What About Up-and-Coming Urban Areas?

I fully expect many of the high-income metropolitan areas just mentioned to remain in the top ten for decades to come. However, over time, some areas will inevitably lose rank as others advance. The million-dollar question is: Which areas will surge up the income rankings next? You may be especially eager to find out if none of the locales on the current list appeal to you.

There are two main factors that indicate if a location will be on the rise or not. The first is educational attainment. The second is type of work. College degrees tend to feed graduates into what are known as knowledge jobs, specifically tech, finance, consulting, and professional services. These industries are a growing portion of the economy and pay high wages. Once an area has job-growth momentum, the momentum tends to continue. More jobs attract more people. More people attract more businesses. More businesses attract better infrastructure. Better infrastructure attracts even more people, and so forth.

If you're currently unhappy with your location and want to continue working, consider setting a relocation milestone. However, before you commit to a specific relocation goal, I recommend you "try before you buy." Spend time exploring your target area in detail on your next vacation. If you like what you see and experience, then try to secure a job there before moving. Relocation has a lot of associated costs, and employment for high-wage roles naturally tends to be quite competitive.

Relocation Costs

On average, Americans move about nine times after the age of eighteen. That's quite a lot, but I believe it. I've already moved ten times between the ages of eighteen and forty-seven, twice in Manhattan and eight times in San Francisco.

Whether you end up moving due to a rent increase, job change, buying a home, starting or ending a relationship, or the desire for more/less, there are costs associated with moving, beyond the price of hauling all your stuff from one place to the other. Some costs are straightforward, like a change in your monthly rent or mortgage. Others are subjective—changes in stress, commute, community, salary, and lifestyle. The best employers are willing to pay their new hires' moving and temporary-lodging costs. Make sure to ask if your relocation costs will be covered before signing a job offer.

Extrapolate how many more times you're likely to move for the rest of your life. Then, estimate how much those moves could set you back and turn that total into a saving goal. If you can incorporate the cost of moving into your finances well in advance, you'll be able to accommodate those additional expenses without derailing your retirement and investment goals. If your relocation plans will improve your finances, then take that leap of faith with confidence. You can always move back if you don't end up enjoying the change.

You don't have to move across the world to a developing country to save money on living expenses. That's too disruptive for most people. The best geoarbitrage strategy is to first *look within your own city*. Moving within the same metropolitan area minimizes disruption and maximizes your cost-savings benefits. You won't have to take a salary hit, either. You'll be surprised how much money you can save by moving just a few short miles away. For example, back in 2014, I moved five miles west in San Francisco and ended up saving about 40 percent on living costs. Everything, from housing to haircuts, was so much cheaper.

If you move to a less densely populated area, the likely benefits include less traffic, less litter, less crime, more greenery, and cheaper goods and services. The more research and testing you can do before relocating the better. The last thing you want to do is uproot your entire life and feel like you made a mistake.

What about geoarbitrage opportunities for remote work? While some industries can function well with remote workers, research shows that, if you're still early in your career, electing to work from home can hinder your career and wage growth. People tend to promote and pay those they like the most. It's simply harder to create a strong connection with your manager and colleagues if you're mostly working remote. Meanwhile, industries that primarily require in-person workforces—such as health care, retail, and hospitality—have been raising wages faster than inflation. If you have the option to work remotely, be aware of the short- and long-term costs and do your research. I'd put your dreams of working remotely full time on hold until you have around ten years of work experience under your belt.

The $20 Million Lottery Ticket

Although hard work and skill are involved in getting rich, putting yourself in the right place might be even more important to maximizing your chances of getting rich. There are plenty of people in the highest-income metropolitan areas who have become incredibly rich just by joining the right firm and sticking with it.

Let me tell you about one of them. In 2018, I started playing pickup softball to make new friends and stay physically active. Although my dreams of playing Major League Baseball died decades ago, for one Saturday morning each week, I could pretend to be a professional baller again. Third base was my favorite position, because I enjoyed the thrill of trying to short-hop rockets and throw runners out at first.

Through softball, I met someone who worked at Uber for three years before the company's initial public offering in 2019. Although Uber's share-price performance was initially disappointing, he still walked away with a couple million dollars, after taxes, through stock options. Not bad for a thirty-year-old.

Several months after Uber's IPO, my friend said he had joined a firm called Figma as a vice president. I had never heard of Figma before, and neither had anybody else. Essentially, Figma makes it easier for designers to design. Okay, cool. But how is that innovative with so many design products out there already?

Well, four years later, I see on the news that Adobe sought to acquire Figma for a whopping $20 billion, and during the 2022 bear market no less. My friend joined when Figma was worth $500 million. Now, his stock options were likely worth more than $40 million. Not bad for a thirty-four-year-old, right? A year later, antitrust regulators nixed the deal, and Figma's value likely declined by half. Still, having roughly $20 million in stock options after only five years is quite an amazing sum.

His $20 million opportunity likely never would have arrived had he not worked in San Francisco. And if I was smarter, I would have asked him, back in 2019, if there was a position for me at his new firm. Oh well, at least we had fun playing softball.

You could be the best person in the world, but if the biggest company in your city doesn't even have a billion-dollar market cap, you might never become a millionaire. Moving to one of the highest-paying or fastest-growing cities, however, can open doors to lucrative networking and investment opportunities.

For instance, despite not having the foresight to join Figma during its early stages, I had the good fortune to invest in Rippling, a human resources and information technology software company, in 2019, when its valuation was only around $270 million. This opportunity arose because I had been playing tennis with a buddy whose business school classmate had recently joined Kleiner Perkins, a venture capital firm. When his friend launched a new fund at Kleiner, I received an invitation to participate. Today, Rippling is valued at more than $10 billion, with the potential for even greater valuation if it continues to execute successfully.

Please don't underestimate the value of being in the right place to increase your chances of making a fortune.

THE *FINANCIAL SAMURAI* WAY

To Contemplate:

☐ Identify the largest, most profitable employers in your current hometown and nearby surrounding area. If there are no significant businesses that could open up a lucrative career path for you, consider relocating.

☐ Think about how many times you've moved so far in your adult life and why. How did each of those changes impact your expenses, lifestyle, social circle, and career?

☐ Extrapolate how many more times you expect to move for the rest of your life. Then, estimate how much those moves could set you back and create a relocation saving goal to fund it.

To Do:

☐ Study the educational attainment level of and type of work available in your current location or any place you want to move to that isn't already a top-income area. Both factors affect how many high-paying jobs there are in the area.

☐ If you want to move to a high-income metropolis, spend time exploring the area in detail. Think about the reasons you wrote down for gaining this wealth and whether the location fits those needs and desires.

☐ Aim to secure a job before relocating, both because of the competitive nature of high-income jobs and to give yourself an easier transition to more expensive living.

☐ Once you enter the workforce in a top-income metro area (the "right place"), build out your network to set yourself up for the next opportunity (the "right time").

☐ Wait to relocate to a lower-income area with a reduced cost of living until after your career is well established or you're ready to retire.

Make the Most of Your Marriage and Family

WHEN YOU'RE FIRST STARTING OUT in your career, your main focus is *you*. But, as time goes on, that focus expands and gets more complex. You may marry, have kids, need to care for your parents, etc.—your focal point shifts from yourself to *them*. As life gets busier, expenses increase, and finding and maintaining balance becomes harder. Your need and desire for money to protect your loved ones increases exponentially.

One way to become a millionaire is to marry into money, which I'll touch on below, but that's not the point of this chapter. Rather, the focus is on having a smarter approach to your finances and strengthening your relationships with your spouse and family. Two people working together to build wealth are usually more effective than just one.

For starters, let's take a step back and talk about the dating scene. There's no denying that the dating world has changed a lot in the last twenty-five to thirty years. Online dating is not only here to stay, it has expanded people's dating pools from just a few neighboring zip codes to entire countries, even reaching across oceans.

While some people have started including financial insights, such as their credit scores, on their dating profiles, most dating-app algorithms filter potential matches based only on personal information and preferences, such as personality, shared interests, religious/political/social views, and swipe history. Those are undoubtably important factors for seekers to find suitable matches, but financial compatibility is way more important to a relationship's long-term success than many people realize. After all, money consistently ranks as a top-three reason why couples fight.

Reasons to Prioritize Your Spouse and Family

If your goal is to become a millionaire, tying the knot with a highly compatible partner might just be your smartest move. Beyond sharing living expenses, the power of dual incomes can turbocharge your household's wealth-building journey. Achieving financial success becomes easier when both of you are rowing in the same direction.

That means avoiding toxic relationships and thinking thrice before marrying someone with bad financial habits. A relationship between a saver, who carefully plans for the future, and a spender, who constantly wants to live in the moment, is unlikely to last. Conversely, a well-matched partnership based on shared financial values will make it much easier for you both to become and stay financially independent while remaining united.

If you're still single and in search of love, *invest as much time in finding a life partner as you do in advancing your career*. Realistically, you have roughly twenty years after high school graduation to discover a soulmate and build a family. While it's possible to find a partner in your forties and beyond, the odds decrease as your dating pool shrinks—the individuals you might be interested in are often already committed by then.

Drop Toxic Relationships

As you embark on the millionaire journey, it's crucial to end any detrimental relationships pronto. Whether they be romantic partners, family, or friends, toxic connections have a knack for exploiting your finances—be it through dependency, control, or outright theft—and degrading your mental health. Cutting these ties is no walk in the park, as they are often entangled in complexities. You might find yourself compelled by love, loyalty, shared history, or blood relations. But remaining in a toxic relationship, even if you believe it's the noble thing to do, is a recipe for long-term disaster. If your relationship thrives on a history of poor decisions and financial abuse, it's time to make a graceful exit.

It's a tough pill to swallow initially, but severing toxic financial ties protects you against the slow bleed of your finances and happiness over the years. Plus, it nudges you toward independence and self-sufficiency, a direction that's in everyone's best interest. It's also worth noting that, once you get to millionaire status, a toxic relationship may get even worse. Instead of being happy for your financial success, your toxic nemesis will likely be envious and secretly want to take you down. When it comes to your financial well-being, guard it with all you've got.

Be Wary of Marrying Someone with Bad Financial Habits

When romance strikes, spotting a partner's faults can be tough. It's as if you have blinders on. If you want your relationship to last over the long term, pay close attention to how your new love spends money—and, hopefully, also saves it.

Any reckless financial habits should give you serious pause. Sure, we've all had an occasional splurge, especially when trying to impress a love interest. But chronic overspending, gambling, and a lack of financial responsibility are all red flags. Alarm bells should be going off in your head if your date has piles of credit card debt, asks to borrow money, routinely pays bills late, has never held a steady job, or has no savings despite a five- or six-figure salary.

Marriage takes work, sometimes a lot of work. If you already see problems with how your partner handles money, or a lack thereof, please heed the experience of all the divorcees out there: tying the knot will only exacerbate preexisting money struggles and give rise to new ones.

The Importance of Shared Financial Goals

Since money is a consistent top-three source of stress in a relationship, I advise you to have serious talks with your partner about money and personal finance before tying the knot. Get financially naked so there are no surprises.

Clarify your financial goals with each other and agree on some big ones, such as when to buy a house, whether to have children, how many children to have, and a target retirement age. If your partner is a financial mess and has opposing financial values, the long-term success of your relationship is at risk.

Misaligned financial goals will lead to resentment and fights. If you have kids together when this happens, that complicates things even further, especially if your plans to pay for your children's education are dashed.

If your partner doesn't show any interest in creating shared financial goals or fails miserably in their efforts to save and invest, don't expect things to magically smooth out once you're married. It's just like that misguided belief that having a baby will fix a troubled couple's relationship problems. The reality is the exact opposite. Becoming a parent amplifies existing relationship problems and likely creates new ones too. Similarly, money problems worsen and get more complicated when you're in a committed relationship.

Discuss your debt, past financial missteps, and your financial aspirations. Only after disclosing everything can you truly build a more fulfilling life together.

Marrying Your Equal Is Better Than Marrying Rich

Now that we've ruled out marrying someone with different financial values, two common ways to marry for greater financial success remain. You can marry your equal, or you can marry rich. In my opinion, marrying your equal is better than marrying rich.

It can be a profound experience when two individuals start from humble beginnings and achieve wealth together. Sudden wealth can be challenging to fully appreciate, particularly if unearned. Conversely, there's immense satisfaction in starting with little, navigating shared struggles side by side, and building a fortune collaboratively.

Imagine meeting your partner in high school or college. Together, you'd endure the challenges of striving for good grades, securing internships, and finding fulfilling jobs. In your twenties, you'd confront betrayals, micromanagement, layoffs, office politics, and other adversities that can strengthen relationships. If you're fortunate, both of you will hit your stride, accumulate wealth, and generously share your success. Experiencing the various stages of personal finance with a partner creates a greater appreciation for money and, more importantly, each other. And, as financial issues recede into the background, you'll have more time to focus on fortifying your relationship.

Two of the main reasons why people break up are a lack of respect followed by resentment. Let's say you're more accomplished than your partner. You may start to lose respect for them if you catch them lounging around too often instead of hustling to get better at something, anything. And if you're the partner who is lounging around, you may start to resent your partner for being so demanding, especially if they are much older than you. Over time, it's easy to take each other for granted.

At my age, I see more relationships fall apart than begin. But, for those that last, the one constant seems to be that the partners are close to equal in accomplishment. That isn't limited to money. People with similar levels of accomplishment tend to be of comparable age, income, education, wealth, and/or experience.

Pros and Cons of Marrying Rich

If you have your sights set on marrying rich, are already pursuing someone significantly wealthier than yourself, or are simply curious about such a relationship, here are my reflections on marrying into money based on extensive reader feedback and observations.

There are four primary advantages to marrying someone wealthy: 1) bypassing a generation of financial struggle, 2) increasing your chances of success, 3) enjoying a luxurious lifestyle, and 4) providing better opportunities for your children. Who doesn't want to access wealth without enduring extreme hardship? Who wouldn't enjoy living at a higher standard while ensuring a comfortable life for their children? Most would sign up for that in a heartbeat.

However, before idealizing the notion of marrying into wealth, consider these four drawbacks: 1) You may constantly feel inadequate; 2) You may face heightened expectations in every aspect of your life; 3) You may be labeled a gold digger; and 4) Your children may crumble under the immense pressure of high expectations or become spoiled and entitled.

Marrying into wealth might also necessitate altering your behavior. In-laws and family friends may raise their standards when evaluating you. If you don't meet their expectations, you could be deemed unworthy. The wealthy are also subject to frequent solicitations for donations, even for causes they don't support, and scrutiny of their spending habits. While having more options seems appealing, an abundance of choices can induce a whole host of negative emotions.

Depending on your spouse for financial support might make you feel like a pawn obliged to suppress your opinions to avoid appearing ungrateful. Not being able to support yourself financially might also make you feel like a child who needs to ask for permission to go outside. Such frustrations can lead to resentment over time.

Furthermore, your children might experience loneliness and depression due to intense competition and a constant sense of inadequacy. Highly successful parents provide many advantages to their children, but being surrounded by success without achieving your own can lead to profound feelings of melancholy and isolation for both you and your children.

Marrying someone who is rich comes with a variety of complications. However, if you happen to have hit the jackpot and think your rich soulmate is fabulous, then congratulations! Make sure money seldom, if ever, comes between the two of you.

Maintain Financial Independence After Getting Married

Depending on someone else for money is an unsettling feeling for most adults. Imagine returning home jobless to live with your parents after four years of college. Not only is your freedom gone and your ego bruised, every time you want to go out to see your friends, you must ask your parents for money to cover transportation, food, and drinks.

Now imagine marrying someone, giving up your job to raise a family, and being entirely dependent on your working spouse for all your spending needs. It's a common situation, but is it ideal? It's one thing to depend on someone for money as a kid. It's another thing to be dependent on someone as an adult.

Modern couples are getting married later and having kids later due to a greater focus on their careers and the higher cost of living. As a result, more couples are bringing large sums of wealth into their marriage than ever before. For all the talk about the desire for financial independence, I find it odd that some couples refuse to establish separate financial accounts to allow each other more freedom. You should be on a shared quest to build your finances together *and* separately. This is the multiplayer approach to money management, in which couples have joint, separate, and private accounts.

Here are the main reasons why each spouse should continue to have their own financial accounts in addition to the couple's joint account.

REASON #1: THE RELEASE VALVE

The desire for independence is strong. It's hard to beat the feeling of being free to do whatever you want with your own money. Separate bank accounts act as release valves for when you don't see eye to eye with your partner on a particular expense. Without one, the chance for argument, and ultimately divorce, increases.

Mental and Muscular Tension

A *Financial Samurai* reader named Lisa reached out to me for advice on how to broach the subject of separate bank accounts with her husband. Three years earlier, she had given up her accounting career and solo bank accounts to raise their two kids full time.

The throes of motherhood were taking a toll on her mind and body, and she desperately wanted to spend $150 for a one-hour massage each month to relax and decompress. Alas, her husband told her it would be a waste of money because he could just give her a massage at home for free.

Over time, little things like this built up resentment in Lisa's mind. Her husband didn't fully grasp the intensity and exhaustion of caring for their baby and toddler around the clock. Meanwhile, her husband was also building resentment because of Lisa's "unnecessary" expenses. He felt she didn't fully appreciate the stress and pressure that weighed on him as the sole income provider for four people.

Small resentments like these are super common among couples with only one income stream and fully combined finances. To help alleviate their tensions, Lisa ultimately decided to open a separate account at the same bank as their joint account so she could withdraw, guilt-free, from the passive income she is now earning on a few CD investments. This small, simple change brought more breathing room and harmony into their day-to-day living.

REASON #2: THE ONGOING FINANCIAL TRAINER

Just like how a personal trainer can push you to do one more set, your spouse can motivate you to earn and save more. Separate financial accounts clearly show where your respective finances stand. Challenge each other to see who can reach the $250,000 crossover point first, or any other amount for that matter. If your starting amounts are vastly different, challenge each other with percentage increases instead.

Your milestone objective is to push each other to achieve optimal financial performance while *concurrently* building a stronger financial life together. If you completely comingle your funds, it's a lot harder to tell exactly how much you've each contributed to the household. Murkiness can lead to laziness and even discontentment.

REASON #3: AN INSURANCE POLICY

Unfortunate events and snafus happen all the time. Such is life. That's all the more reason to be prepared and diversified. Identity theft, hacked accounts, Ponzi schemes, bank runs, divorce, probate complications, life insurance claim delays, you name it—these and more have caught plenty of people by surprise.

Having separate bank accounts, especially at different financial institutions, can provide not only easier access to cash when you need it most but also added security. Deposits are insured up to $250,000 per depositor, per FDIC-insured bank, per ownership category. During the 2008 global financial crisis, having a diversification of bank accounts proved to be a relief for couples with significant assets. It's worth taking advantage of such diversification as your wealth grows.

Help a Stay-at-Home Spouse Stay Financially Independent

Although many married couples are dual income, you may be a single-income household now or at some point in the future. How can a stay-at-home spouse earn money if they don't have a job? Well, that's easy. They don't need to if you value their role.

Being a stay-at-home parent is easily worth *at least* your city's median income. If you disagree, take the number of hours the stay-at-home spouse cares for your kids and multiply it by the average hourly cost for day care or a nanny. That is the amount of money their contribution is worth and how much they deserve to make, save, and spend. If you're a stay-at-home parent, please don't short-change your contributions. Economically, you are contributing far more than you may realize.

From a cash-flow perspective, it may not be feasible for many couples to have one parent stay at home. However, for those that do, I recommend earmarking at least some amount of money for the primary caregiver to invest and have at their disposal each month so they can spend freely without guilt. After all, they're caring for your most precious assets.

Other Ways to Reach Spousal Financial Independence

Sign a prenuptial agreement. Although it's not a romantic topic, a generous prenuptial agreement can protect the less wealthy spouse in case of a divorce and be customized as you see fit. The longer the marriage, the more financially at risk nonworking spouses become as their skills and networks become outdated. The greater the net-worth difference before marriage, the greater the importance of a prenuptial agreement.

For example, one couple I know has a prenuptial agreement where the man, an entrepreneur whose net worth is more than $50 million, agreed to pay his wife $2 million if they divorce within five years through no fault of his own. His wife's net worth was worth only $200,000, so the prenuptial agreement seems like a fair deal.

Marriage is the biggest transaction of your life, and prenups are essential to protect both of you. Postnuptial agreements—similar to prenups, but signed *after* the wedding—are also worth considering, so both of you will know how to separate your assets and debts in the case of a divorce.

Contribute extra to your spouse's retirement accounts.
If one spouse has less saved for retirement, the other spouse can give them a boost to create more balance. You can't fund someone else's 401(k), but you can help build up your spouse's after-tax investment accounts.

Pay down your spouse's debt. Helping to pay down your spouse's credit card and/or student loan debt upon entering a marriage is a very generous gesture. Even if the income imbalance persists, the spouse whose debt was paid off will feel incredibly liberated and appreciative.

Secure your children's financial needs. Even if your marriage doesn't make it, it's important that your children are taken care of. This means writing a will, funding a 529 college savings plan, opening a custodial Roth IRA, setting up a revocable living trust, owning term life insurance policies, and creating a death file.* Your spouse naturally becomes more financially independent when they no longer have to worry about your children's finances.

Create a SLAT (Spousal Lifetime Access Trust). A SLAT is an irrevocable trust into which one spouse deposits gifts to benefit the other spouse (and, potentially, other family members) while removing those assets from the combined estate. Appreciation on the transferred assets is not subject to estate taxes.

Remember, as a couple you want to set and achieve financial milestones together while also ensuring neither spouse ever loses financial freedom. Giving someone financial independence is a gift of love.

---

* Please see Milestone 12 and the Further Reading section at the end of the book for links to helpful articles I've written on these topics.

College Sweethearts

Ever since I first crossed paths with her at the College of William & Mary, I've harbored the desire to give my wife the world. I recognized early on that she was my life partner, and I owe her a tremendous debt of gratitude for standing by me since our days as cash-strapped college students.

When I pursued a job in New York City during my senior year, she woke up at 5:30 a.m. to make sure I didn't oversleep for my seven a.m. interviews. I was subsequently able to clear her last college loan after my third year of work and purchase a house in San Francisco to enhance our quality of life.

Our bond is unique because financial considerations never played a pivotal role in our relationship. Our idea of a lovely date night involved using our meal cards to enjoy some rubber-chicken dinners and a milkshake at the campus cafeteria.

I take pride in my wife's financial independence. She has never required direct financial assistance from me. She carved out a successful thirteen-year career in finance, and she negotiated a severance package in 2014, liberating herself from the confines of traditional corporate life. Since then, we have continued to build our wealth, both collectively and individually.

Knowing that my wife possesses her own robust financial reserves brings me immense peace of mind. I am reassured that, when I pass, she will thrive independently.

Cherish Your Compatibility

As much as I wish I could relay a magic formula for how to find a highly compatible partner, there isn't one. Every online dating app claims to have the best matching algorithm, but there are too many unquantifiable and subjective factors that affect whether or not two people will ultimately hit it off. This is why dating reality shows, like *Love Is Blind*, are so addictive to watch—human interaction is so incredibly unpredictable and entertaining to observe.

What I can say is that genuine friendship is what a long-lasting marriage needs to have at its core to be sustainable. Next in line is having each other's backs through both the good and the bad as well as having shared values.

If you're fortunate enough to find someone you want to marry or cohabitate with, count yourself lucky. Cherish your compatibility and be prepared to put in the work after the honeymoon phase is over. The longevity of your marriage and the success of your financial future depend on it.

Aim for the Three *H*s: Health, Happiness, and Harmony

When it comes to marriage, prioritize what I dub the three *H*s: health, happiness, and harmony. First and foremost, health must take precedence. By that, I'm referring to physical, mental, and emotional health. When one partner is feeling sick, burned out, or anxious about something, the other must step up. Nothing else matters when your health goes. The key is to restore balance as quickly as possible so you both don't end up down for the count simultaneously.

As for happiness, it is mostly a choice. But it is also much easier to acquire and sustain if you and your spouse are communicating well. Support each other and be on the same page financially. Recognize each other's contributions so you both feel appreciated. This breeds harmony. Having health, happiness, and harmony in your marriage is like hitting a trifecta.

If there's dissonance in your marriage, don't let it fester. Have difficult conversations and work through uncomfortable or painful moments head-on. If you're unable to have effective conversations and fail to come up with suitable solutions to your problems together, invest in marriage counseling. Yes, counseling can be expensive, but it's well worth it to have a neutral mediator who can help you navigate forward. Plus, it's a heck of a lot cheaper than divorce.

If things still don't resolve after therapy, at least you'll have no regrets about not having tried your best. You can then figure out how to part ways toward a hopefully more peaceful future.

The Difficulties and Costs of Divorce

Speaking of divorce, although it is prevalent in the US, way more people get married each year than divorced—nearly 1.3 million more. Nobody goes into a marriage expecting it to end in divorce, but roughly 40 percent of first marriages end in divorce, and the average marriage lasts just eight years.

Interestingly, there is a correlation between household income and the likelihood of divorce. Couples making less than $200,000 have around a 40 percent chance of their marriages dissolving. But once household income levels cross over the $200,000 mark, that percentage drops down to 30 percent, and then again to 25 percent around $600,000. However, the rate climbs back up to 30 percent for households making more than $600,000.

Perhaps the approach to $1 million brings additional lifestyle complications, such as heightened work stress and less time to devote to each other. After all, the number one reason for divorce is lack of commitment. Thus, the closer you get to millionaire status, the more important it is to remember to appreciate, communicate with, and support your partner. And don't forget to have fun together with all that money you're hard at work accumulating.

Eight Ways to Strengthen Your Marriage

Here are eight ongoing practices you can utilize in your marriage to help it stay strong, supported, and balanced.

1. **Validate your partner.** The happiest couples not only listen to each other, they also show they truly understand *why* the other feels the way they do. Show kindness and recognize effort.

2. **Develop an outside support group of your own friends and colleagues.** Friends help alleviate the pressure placed on your partner to constantly support you.

3. **Create boundaries that separate work from home.** Everybody has bad days at work, but don't take those frustrations out on your loved ones.

4. **Forgive and ask for forgiveness.** Successful marriages resolve conflict fairly and with respect. This requires admitting fault, being vulnerable, understanding each other's points of view, and finding common ground.

5. **Consider keeping both separate and joint finances.** This approach gives each partner more flexibility and independence in spending money.

6. **Know thyself.** When you understand your own annoyances and what propels you forward, you can improve how you communicate with your partner. This leads to a stronger and more harmonious relationship. You will also be able to take better care of yourself.

7. **Accept there will be turbulence.** No relationship is perfect. Expect difficult times so you are better prepared and more open to compromise. Use conflict as a way to learn and to improve your marriage. When problems arise, find solutions as a team.

8. **Lean in to each other's bids for connection.** Bids are those little and big attempts to connect that show you care about each other and genuinely enjoy spending time together.

Even in the event of divorce, there's hope for a brighter future. It's possible to emerge from the experience stronger and happier. People often start anew after a divorce and ultimately become more empowered. The grim tales of divorce wreaking havoc on people's finances, however, are not unfounded. Divorce can be a devastating experience financially and emotionally and, if things get out of control, may cause you to give up on your dreams for years.

One of my longtime *Financial Samurai* readers shared his harrowing experience, in which his ex-wife's vindictiveness decimated his entire net worth of $1.1 million. After enduring thirteen months of anguish and financial strain, he found himself not only financially ruined but also burdened with more than $300,000 in his own legal fees and another $100,000 for his ex-wife's lawyers.

Remarkably, he refused to be defeated and embarked on a journey of recovery. Through disciplined saving and frugal living, he managed to claw his way back from the depths of despair. Four years after his divorce, he was debt-free, and he continues to rebuild his financial foundation. His story epitomizes the power of perseverance in overcoming adversity. But there are always two sides to every story.

Invest in Your Children

Life can be more joyous with children, but also a lot more complicated and exhausting in the early years. Before having children, my wife and I hardly ever fought. Once we had our son, in 2017, the constant stress and anxiety we felt as first-time parents made us bicker more frequently. Get your finances in order before having children, because if you can't take care of yourself first, it becomes much harder to invest in your children's futures.

How do you make the most of your relationship with your children? Spend as much quality time with them as you can. Convey support and excitement about their interests. Explain why things are the way they are instead of just telling them they are so. Show up for them when it counts the most. Your children don't care about how much money you have if their basic needs are taken care of. What they care about most is whether you're present in their lives.

Surprisingly, as important as financial literacy is as a life skill, it's still not a required subject in most schools. I implore you to be sure they know the basics *before* you send them off on their own. After all, they can have the fanciest degrees in the world and still struggle in life if they don't get their money right.

Think about the eighteen years your children live at home with you as an opportunity to teach them everything you know. This includes making them as financially literate as possible so they can figure out their finances on their own once they leave. These fundamentals, paired with their own education in adulthood, will help them achieve true wealth and prevent them from boomeranging back into your basement. The clock is ticking.

Planning for your child's education is not something to downplay or put off, either. For example, the average cost of tuition and fees for four years at a public college is about $43,000 today. At a private college it's $169,000. By the year 2042, those costs could easily surpass $250,000 and $500,000, respectively. Some of the top private universities could easily cost more than $1 million over four years by then.

College may not carry as much importance in the future, and not every career will require a four-year degree, but research shows that higher education correlates strongly with boosted lifetime earnings. Not only will your children likely make more money as college graduates, they may also live longer and experience increased happiness.

By starting early, estimating future costs, and saving consistently from your child's birth through their teenage years, you can contribute significantly to their higher education. Every dollar saved reduces their potential on student debt and thereby sets them up for greater financial success after graduation. See the Further Reading section for tips on how to save for your child's education.

What About Your Aging Parents?

Middle-aged individuals have many responsibilities these days. They're still raising their kids, but their parents require more and more attention due to health concerns. Being stuck in this sandwich comes with a lot of responsibility and can put strain on even the strongest of marriages and families.

If you're lucky, your parents are still thriving physically, mentally, and financially. But there likely will come a time when one or both of them, along with your spouse's parents, will need help in one or more of those capacities. If you're still supporting your own children when this happens and/or are completely unprepared, it could jeopardize your own financial and mental health. To avoid that pitfall, watch out for these three things:

1. **Shrinking retirement funds.** The infamous golden parachute isn't what it used to be. Pensions are rare now, Social Security is underfunded, and most retirees have not picked up the slack with their 401(k) accounts. As a result, your parents may need you to step in and cover their expenses. To find out how they are doing financially, ask them. If you need to coax them into revealing their financial secrets, it may be easier over a bottle of fine wine.

2. **You may be on the hook for your parents' long-term care costs.** Planning for long-term care is not a fun conversation, yet close to 70 percent of people sixty-five and older will need it at some point. It's incredibly expensive, running anywhere from about $2,050 per month for adult day care to $9,700 per month for a private room in a nursing home, with prices expected to increase annually at a faster rate than inflation. Because it's an emotional and stressful transition, many people don't realize that, when they admit a parent into a facility, they are signing financial responsibility for them should the parent run out of money to pay the bills. Because this can put your financial well-being at risk, it is worthwhile to research long-term care insurance and to talk to a lawyer about options to protect your own assets, such as establishing power of attorney.

3. **Career delays and missed advancement opportunities.** Elder care can require many hours and even more patience. If you need to step in, a short leave of absence from work may be fine, but a long time away could impede your career growth. Get a contingency plan in place for your parents' care long before you need it. Even if things change, some preparation is better than none.

Our parents took care of us for the first eighteen years of our lives. As dutiful children, we should take care of them for at least the last eighteen years of theirs.

THE *FINANCIAL SAMURAI* WAY

To Contemplate:

☐ If you're seeking a romantic partner, compare the qualities you're really looking for against the matching criteria your dating app is using. Don't underestimate the importance of financial compatibility.

☐ Shared financial values, goals, and habits make it easier to achieve financial success and stay united as a couple over the long haul.

☐ Consider the benefits of marrying an equal and building your fortune together. Marrying rich may sound alluring, but there are many negatives to contemplate.

To Do:

☐ Take your blinders off when you're dating someone. Pay close attention to how they make, spend, and save their money. If they have reckless financial habits, do yourself a favor and part ways amicably.

☐ Let go of toxic relationships for the best interest of your financial and mental well-being.

☐ If you find someone you're highly compatible with, have three or more lengthy discussions with them about their detailed finances long before you get engaged.

☐ Set three to five specific financial milestones with your partner and achieve one or two of them before getting married. Challenge each other to see who can reach the $250,000 mark more quickly. Exchange ideas for businesses.

☐ Maintain both separate and joint financial accounts after you get married. For financial peace of mind, build wealth both together and separately.

☐ Sign a prenup if your net worth is significantly different than your partner's.

☐ Prioritize the three *H*s in your marriage. If there's dissonance in your relationship, sit down together once a week and talk through your challenges head-on. Seek help from a therapist or mediator if you're stuck or going into decline.

☐ Invest in your children by showing up when it counts and taking an active role in their education. Teach them the fundamentals of financial literacy before they turn eighteen.

☐ Start saving for your child's education early and often. There are many lifestyle and financial benefits to higher education.

☐ Prepare to take care of your parents for the last years of their lives. It is our responsibility as Financial Samurai.

Legacy—The Millionaire's Everlasting Imprint

THERE'S NO POINT IN WORKING YOURSELF TO EXHAUS-tion only to die early because you failed to take care of your health. Nor is it worth hustling to get rich by your fifties only to end up broke by age sixty because you got too carried away with spending your fortune.

In this section, I'll talk about the important concept of con-sumption smoothing and teach you how to calculate how much to spend during the remainder of your days so you don't die with way too much or far too little. Using a dynamic withdrawal rate can also help protect what you've worked so hard to achieve, especially in extreme times. That way, if the economy decides to fall apart when you're fifty-nine or shoots to the moon when you're sixty-eight, you'll know exactly what to do.

I'll also share some fun ways to spend your wealth sensibly and highlight additional milestones that can help increase your longevity so you can enjoy your wealth for longer. Then, I'll round things off with my thoughts on why you need to take care of estate planning now. Even though you may not feel it yet, legacy increases in importance as we age. Use this opportunity to start thinking about how you want to leave your mark on the world.

Spend Your Wealth Judiciously

SO, YOU'VE CRACKED MILLIONAIRE STATUS—CONGRATS! Now the real question looms: What will become of the fortune you've amassed? Unless you are a strict minimalist and genuinely want everything you ever earned and own to go to your beneficiaries, there's little point in accumulating wealth if you never enjoy it. After all, the crowning milestone is living an extraordinary life, not having an extraordinary bank account balance that's destined to spur future family feuds.

Imagine depriving yourself of love, adventure, and rest—all sacrificed during years of seemingly endless sixty-hour workweeks spent chasing the millionaire dream. For what? So one day your heirs can bicker over assets you never felt comfortable enough to spend on your own happiness? Talk about a lousy deal and a poor use of your time and energy. You really shouldn't have stressed so much about that poor investment or subpar performance review at work.

Good Judgment Is Key When Decumulating Wealth

Altering the lifelong frugality that got you here can prove tricky. Every choice becomes a mental cost-benefit wrestling match. Long-standing financial habits and an accumulator's mindset can be harder to shake than you might expect.

Imagine having to evaluate every expenditure against potential savings and earnings lost. Be careful—left unchecked, the thirst for perpetual wealth accumulation can consume you entirely. Yet, we've also heard countless stories of people who lost their fortunes practically overnight because they got carried away or took on too much risk. Since the main point of building wealth is to be able to spend it on yourself and what you value the most, sensible spending decisions are not only important today but all the way through to your last days.

As we approach the last milestone, I want to give you some guidance about how much to spend throughout the rest of your life along with some responsible and fun ways to decumulate your wealth. The possibilities are endless.

Figuring Out How Much More Money to Spend

Whether we like it or not, that infamous grim reaper will come calling one day. His morbid deadline requires important math from the millionaire set. Your milestone mission, if you choose to accept it, is to embrace the art of responsible consumption smoothing.

Consumption smoothing means mastering how to spend your money more *evenly* throughout your life, rather than just at the very end, to improve the overall quality of your lifestyle over a longer span of years. Specifically, you can calculate a maximum annual spending amount that will enable you to fade to black with zero left over.

The math is simple. Tally your liquid net worth, then divide it by your life expectancy minus your current age. For example, a fifty-year-old woman with a $1.45 million net worth and an estimated lifespan of seventy-nine could withdraw roughly $50,000 annually ($1.45M / (79 − 50) = $50,000) to arrive at the pearly gates with her account balances drawn down to nil.

Of course, her annual drawdown amount will require adjusting for any active or passive income still trickling in and any large, one-off expenses going out. In addition, there are investment-return considerations to estimate. But the goal of this simple calculation is to come up with a baseline minimum to spend each year.

Let's say the same fifty-year-old has $100,000 in after-tax wage earnings plus another $10,000 in after-tax investment income coming in each year. She would have to spend $160,000 annually (not $50,000) to siphon away the $50,000 net worth chunk plus those sources of income.

The problem is, she's accustomed to spending only $80,000 a year after-tax. Increasing her spending by 100 percent, to $160,000, will feel mighty uncomfortable to a capital accumulator conditioned to scrimp and save. Hence, the inertia of underspending impedes millionaires' best plans to die with nothing. The wealth snowball grows and rolls downhill faster than most people's intended withdrawals can melt it away.

However, if you practice consumption smoothing at an earlier age, you won't have to increase your spending by so drastic an amount.

The 4 Percent Rule vs. a Dynamic
Safe Withdrawal Rate

Another easy way to determine how much you can afford to spend in retirement is to follow the 4 percent rule. It states that you can withdraw 4 percent of your liquid net worth (investments) each year and not worry about running out of money before you die. The rule was formulated by Bill Bengen in the 1990s, when the risk-free rate of return (the ten-year Treasury bond yield) was closer to 6 percent. If you had a relatively conservative portfolio returning close to 6 percent, you wouldn't run out of money if you withdrew 4 percent annually. I actually hosted a wonderful interview with Bill on my podcast you can take a listen to.[*]

Instead of blindly following the 4 percent rule from decades ago, consider a dynamic safe-withdrawal approach—the *Financial Samurai* Withdrawal Rate (or FSWR for all you acronym lovers). It links spending to bond yields using this formula:

FSWR = 80% × 10-Year Treasury Rate

For example, if the ten-year bond yield is at 4 percent, consider withdrawing at a 3.2 percent rate. If you have $1 million in investments, that means withdrawing about $32,000 a year to spend. You're unlikely to have your entire investment portfolio or net worth in risk-free Treasury bonds, but they don't have to be. The ten-year Treasury bond yield is a golden figure that bakes in current and expected inflation, risk appetite, expected returns for risk assets, and economic forecasts.

If the ten-year Treasury bond yield drops to 1 percent, because the economy is falling apart and investors are rushing to the safety of Treasuries, consider lowering your safe-withdrawal rate to just

---

[*] financialsamurai.com/bill-bengen-retire-earlier

0.8 percent so you can conserve capital for emergencies or invest more in the stock market and other risk assets. You may even want to earn some supplemental income if you have a cash-flow shortfall.

Conversely, if the ten-year bond yield rises to 5 percent due to elevated inflation, consider withdrawing at a 4.8 percent rate in order to spend more today, since your purchasing power is weakening. Of course, risk assets could also come tumbling down due to overly restrictive interest rates slowing down growth. It's up to you to constantly monitor your personal economic situation and your country's overall economic situation to make the best spending choices possible.

By adopting FSWR plus my simple consumption smoothing calculation on spending your net worth down to zero, you can get a great idea of how much more you need to decumulate. It won't be easy to find that ideal spending balance, but it's worth it to try. Go back to the time when you worked for a micromanager that made your life hell for years. Recall the fear you had about putting your hard-earned money into a risky investment that ultimately paid off. Now honor your younger self's sacrifices by boosting your spending for a better life today.

Find a Happy Balance Between Giving and Receiving

Being financially comfortable does have its benefits. One of the things I've come to appreciate is the ability to be more generous with both my time and money. Giving is a heck of a lot more satisfying than receiving. It's a large part of the reason why I've been publishing three free posts a week on *Financial Samurai* since July 2009. Being able to guide a reader through a financial problem or entertain a stranger who is having a bad day feels wonderful. But I wouldn't have been able to keep up this rigorous publishing schedule if I didn't have enough passive income to cover my basic living expenses.

Find ways to help others more often with whatever spare resources you have. Do not let the knowledge and wisdom you've accumulated die with you. Instead, do your best to teach as many people as possible. If you can, you'll find more meaning and purpose in your life, and your happiness will increase.

The next question to ask yourself is: What will I do with all the superfluous wealth I've accumulated? Sure, you *could* give it all away. But, going back to what I said before, balance is key. Go back and revisit the purposes and goals for your wealth that you wrote down at the start of the book. Now it's time to execute. Here are some thoughts on how to spend your money.

Ideas for Spending Your Millions

Never fear, my fun ideas for spending down your millions are here.

Lavish Generosity and Tipping

Embrace extravagant tipping to embody a real-life fairy godmother or Santa Claus. Leave servers speechless with gratuities exceeding 30 percent.

Support aspiring entrepreneurs by funding their start-up dreams through micro-grants and angel investing. While some investments may falter, others could yield significant returns.

Give back to your loved ones while you're still alive. If your family knows you're financially secure, consider sharing your blessings with those closest to you. Once you've won the financial lottery, share your winnings with the many people you love.

Parties to Remember Forever

When it comes to spending money, luxury items like watches and cars may have appeal initially, but their allure fades over time. Instead, invest some of your splurge funds in creating lasting memories.

Host unforgettable theme parties, arrange exclusive wine tastings or cooking classes with renowned chefs, or indulge in custom-designed attire for special occasions. Find reasons to celebrate and feel joy.

The memories you share with friends become more precious over time. And true friends will cherish your generosity, reciprocating with invites to their own memorable events.

Take Your Friends on Luxurious Vacations

Why attend the Super Bowl or a Taylor Swift concert by yourself if you can afford to be surrounded by friends? Treat your best buds to front-row or box seats and make everlasting memories while getting in on all the action.

Similarly, you can invite your friends on an all-expenses-paid trip to the French Riviera or Bora Bora. Rent a beachfront house so you can all chill under one roof and party into the night together.

While you're at it, book the best activities the locale has to offer and cross some items off your bucket lists. Indulge in first-class dining or go on an exclusive photo safari. Treat these experiences as investments in your happiness bank. I promise you, they will appreciate in value.

The Dream Home

If the idea of tossing cash around like confetti gives you the jitters, fear not. The easiest way to responsibly spend down your fortune is to purchase an amazing primary residence.

Think about it—the average person spends at least twelve hours a day at home. If you're lucky enough to work from home or are savoring retirement, that number could easily rise to twenty hours or more. Your home is practically your second skin, your most used and cherished asset. So why not own the nicest one you can afford?

Go for that killer view with a huge patio to host soirées. Or lock in a sprawling piece of land where your kids or furry friends can frolic for hours on end. Your dream, your rules.

Of course, don't spend more than you can manage. Otherwise, your daily stress level will skyrocket, and your current and future finances could get all out of whack. To make yourself feel better after each property tax payment and maintenance expense, tell yourself these costs are helping you decumulate for the ultimate lifestyle today.

Invest in Your Health

Can you imagine finally hitting that coveted $1 million net worth milestone after decades of grinding away, only to kick the bucket the following week? Talk about cosmic injustice.

Now, consider this alternative—becoming a millionaire by fifty and relishing a healthy lifestyle for the next four decades. Far more appealing, right? Enjoying the fruits of your success isn't just about spending money, it's also about embracing the art of living a long time.

The Free Way to Live Longer

As practical millionaires, let's explore how we can extend our lifespans for free.

If you want to increase your chances of living a longer and

healthier life, dive into the blue zones, a term coined by Dan Buettner. In Dan's insightful documentary and book, he unravels the extraordinary longevity found in five distinct regions—Sardinia, Italy; Okinawa, Japan; the Nicoya Peninsula in Costa Rica; Ikaria, Greece; and Loma Linda, California. These pockets of exceptional health boast an unusually high number of centenarians—people who are one hundred or more years old—who defy the conventional aging process and sidestep major health issues. These communities thrive on a holistic approach to well-being, recognizing that it's the collective impact of multiple lifestyle factors that contribute to their extraordinary health.

One of the cornerstones of blue-zone living is a primarily plant-based diet rich in beans. This dietary choice is coupled with a reduction in beef and dairy consumption and a preference for herbal tea and red wine, beverages recognized for their antioxidant-rich properties, particularly Cannonau wine in Sardinia.

Beyond dietary practices, blue zones emphasize the importance of community and social connections. They counter loneliness, a silent epidemic that can dramatically impact life expectancy, by fostering close-knit social circles, improving mental health, and building a strong sense of *ikigai*—a Japanese term that translates as "a reason to live." Living a life filled with purpose and joy is a key component of blue-zone communities.

An intriguing aspect of blue-zone living is the incorporation of daily walks. In Okinawa, Ikaria, and Sardinia, the terrain naturally encourages walking, resulting in low-impact exercise and opportunities for social interactions. Joining a walking group not only adds accountability to fitness routines, it strengthens social bonds, and it doesn't cost a thing. This enhances your potential for a longer and healthier life. If you can't find a walking group, consider getting a dog, who will eagerly join you on any journey out of the house.

The blue-zone lifestyle is not just a prescription for physical health, it's a holistic guide to overall well-being. By integrating the wisdom of these exceptional communities, we can embark on a transformative journey toward increased vitality, purpose, and the promise of a more fulfilling and extended life. Although I can't outright guarantee you'll live longer by embracing these practices, I'm confident you will increase your odds.

Six Ways to Spend Your Way to Better Health

Now let's dive into how you can spend money to potentially live healthier and longer.

1) HEALTH SCANS ($100–$2,500)

Advancements in biotechnology are helping people identify health problems faster and more accurately than ever before. Thus, in your milestone quest to both live longer and spend your wealth, consider getting an elite package of health testing each year to catch issues early. These can include heart scans, biomarker bloodwork, genetics testing, cancer screening, and more.

These health scans are usually not covered by insurance and can run into the thousands of dollars, but they could literally add years onto your life thanks to early detection. Today, full-body scans for cancer have the ability to detect insidious cancer cells before they metastasize. Their usage is currently deemed controversial in the medical community due to their debatable efficacy and the ramifications of false positives and radiation. Much research and development is still underway. Nevertheless, health scans can already provide a lot of information in the right circumstances. Who knows what they'll potentially be able to uncover ten or twenty years from now.

Here are some examples of the available health scans today and their approximate costs. Check with your doctor to understand any possible side effects and to get the latest updates on these continually developing technologies.

Whole-body scan ($2,499). Comprehensive full-body scans can differentiate malignant cancer from benign conditions, such as cysts, hematomas, hemangiomas, and abscesses, among other things.

DEXA or DXA scan ($100–$300). These scans are primarily used to measure bone density to help identify your risk of breaking a bone. They're often used to help diagnose bone-related health problems, such as osteoporosis, or to assess your risk of getting them. DEXA scans can also be used for insights on body fat, visceral fat, muscle mass, and muscle imbalance asymmetries.

Galleri test ($950). Biotech company GRAIL created the Galleri test using MCED (multi-cancer early detection) technologies that can detect more than fifty types of cancer through a simple blood test even before symptoms are present.

If you get one or more of these scans, be aware that there is a risk of false positives and false negatives. In other words, a scan may conclude you have cancer when you really don't, and vice versa. The resulting emotional stress and subsequent testing may be costly. Hence, before getting any body scans or testing, you may want to ask yourself if you really want to know how long you might have left to live. If you don't, you might as well try to live every day like it's your last.

2) CONCIERGE DOCTORS ($5,000–$50,000 PER YEAR)

Step into the world of the ultrarich, where concierge doctors, also known as private doctors, redefine the health-care experience.

Offering a direct line of communication through emails and mobile devices, these full-service doctors provide immediate assistance whenever you have a question or concern. Say goodbye to six-month waitlists for a simple checkup. Concierge doctors provide preferential appointment scheduling, the flexibility of last-minute examinations, easier access to vaccinations and medicines in low supply, and some even do house calls.

3) PERSONAL TRAINERS ($50-$200 PER HOUR)

Embarking on a fitness journey with a personal trainer is like unlocking a customized road map to success. Not only do they bring expertise to the table, they can also tailor workouts specifically to your body, goals, and limitations. They also act as a constant source of motivation and accountability to help you safely push past your limits while minimizing injury. As we get older, our minds tend to outlast our bodies. If we're not careful, we might push our bodies beyond their true capabilities.

4) PRIVATE CHEFS ($500-$3,500 PER MONTH)

Indulging in the services of a personal chef is a game changer when it comes to eating healthier. Beyond the obvious perk of savoring mouthwatering meals in correct portion sizes, hiring a personal chef also frees up time and energy. Instead of feeling the burden of everything from meal planning to cleaning up a messy kitchen, you can happily focus on whatever you want. If a private chef is too much, you can always order food delivery from one of your favorite restaurants instead. What carnivore doesn't enjoy the occasional twenty-eight-day dry-aged ribeye or some toro sashimi?

5) MENTAL WELL-BEING ACTIVITIES ($50-$5,000)

Mental health is just as vital as physical health, yet society still struggles to fully recognize its importance. We invest heavily in fitness trainers, nutritionists, and doctors, but when it comes to addressing our mental anguish, we often hesitate to seek support from therapists who can help heal our traumas and emotional wounds. If you're feeling mentally unwell, consider hiring a therapist or a life coach to nurture your soul and cheer you on.

If you need a refreshing break, think about wellness retreats focused on relaxation and self-discovery. Engaging in personal development workshops or exploring new creative hobbies—such as painting, writing, or playing music—can provide a wonderful outlet for self-expression and resilience. Together, these activities create a holistic approach to enhancing your mental health and overall happiness.

6) PRIVATE SPORTS CLUBS ($30-$500 PER MONTH PLUS AN INITIATION FEE OF UP TO $300,000)

What's my go-to wellness splurge? A membership at a private sports club. Sports clubs like mine are not just fancy gyms. They are havens where you can break a sweat, indulge in sports, mingle with friends, and genuinely feel at home. Plus, having access to indoor facilities in the winter is a fantastic remedy for seasonal affective disorder (SAD).

Private sports clubs are also a gateway to a network of friendships. The more connections you make, the more unforeseen and advantageous opportunities you may encounter. For example, a fellow member might transform into a valuable client during a tennis match, or that pickleball buddy who's on the school board of a dream school might be the golden admissions ticket for your child's next educational adventure.

You'll Still Likely Die with Too Much Money

Even if you tick your way through my spending suggestions, you could still end up with excess assets, especially if you're a die-hard saver who has accumulated a large financial nut. Long-standing financial habits are hard to change after decades of accumulating. Having interviewed more than a thousand millionaires since 2009, I have discovered that many are psychologically unable to splurge. Functionally, they remain constrained by an accumulator's mindset, which can sometimes feel like a cage.

As you embark on the journey of spending down your wealth, it's crucial to approach decumulation with the same level of intentionality as you did accumulating wealth. Don't let a month pass without reaching your spending target. Just as you systematically increased your saving rate during the wealth accumulation phase, allocate a percentage for spending and incrementally raise it over time.

For instance, in the first half of the year, aim to spend 10 percent more than usual to ease into the process. Then, in the latter half, increase your spending by 20 percent. By adopting this intentional approach, you'll achieve smoother consumption patterns over your lifetime.

Celebrate your success as you navigate the path of decumulation.

To Contemplate:

☐ Consider the various ramifications of inaccurate medical results before diving into disease-detection testing and body scans. Preventative care through annual physicals is important, especially after the age of forty. However, if you're already self-motivated to live your best life today, then perhaps there's no need to test fate with a health scan.

☐ Ask yourself how you'd feel if you died with millions of unspent dollars? Now ask your thirty-five-year-old self how they'd feel if you didn't spend down or give away your wealth while living.

To Do:

☐ Revisit the purposes and goals you set for your millionaire journey at the start of this book. Think about how you might change them with the knowledge you've gained and the spending ideas presented in this chapter.

☐ Practice consumption smoothing to balance spending throughout your life for an enhanced quality of life over more years.

☐ Determine your baseline spending by calculating your liquid net worth, then divide it by life expectancy minus your current age. Use this figure as the minimum amount you should be spending each year for decumulation.

☐ Invest in an exceptional primary residence. A well-chosen home can be both a significant consumption item and potential appreciation asset.

☐ Use a dynamic withdrawal rate, such as FSWR, to adapt with changing times.

☐ Give your time and resources to others without asking for anything in return. There's no greater way to feel happy than to help others.

☐ Study the secrets of the blue zones and prioritize spending on health improvements if you want to increase your chances of living a longer and more robust life.

Create an Immortal Legacy

HAVE YOU EVER WONDERED WHY the ultra-wealthy donate tens or hundreds of millions of dollars to elite universities with enormous endowments? Surely institutions like Harvard, which has more than $50 billion in its coffers, don't actually need such sums.

The answer lies in legacy.

I used to consider the ostentatious legacy-building of financial donors rather distasteful. Inscribing one's name on a wooden bench seemed silly. However, having entered my late forties, mortality feels nearer. I don't have the means to legally bribe my children's way into an elite university with a new *Financial Samurai* wing, but perhaps I can author works with staying power. If I write wisely and sincerely, my books may also stand the test of time.

Why Legacy Matters

There are many ways to bestow legacy, from small, private mementos to colossal, public displays. As I'll discuss, you can let your imagination run wild and customize your legacy to your heart's content.

It's also important to ensure that your family and loved ones are both protected and well cared for after you pass. Estate planning may not be the most comfortable task, but it's a crucial aspect of your millionaire journey. For what it's worth, once you get your affairs in order, you'll sleep a lot better at night.

You Too Will Crave Legacy

Seeking to establish an enduring legacy is part of human nature. Even if immortalizing your name doesn't appeal to you now, it eventually will. As death approaches, the longing to leave something memorable behind creeps in, even if that something is as humble as your prized comic book collection.

Some manifest legacy through their children. Raising good-hearted, well-adjusted kids who make positive contributions to the world is every parent's fundamental wish. Hence, those generational naming conventions—little John IV!

Those without children still have countless options to cement their legacies. Here are some ideas:

- Publish a book of your recipes, life lessons, or family history.

- Fund public art installations, park benches, or paving stones to get your family's name engraved on commemorative plaques.

- Establish annual university scholarships in your name.

- Purchase beloved green spaces and nature preserves via conservation trusts. Your environmental gift will thrive for generations.

- Create a website, podcast, YouTube channel, or personal video journal to chronicle your innermost thoughts and feelings so they can be cherished indefinitely.

When our time comes, may we rest in peace knowing that we contributed something meaningful to the world. And, if there is an afterlife, we can look down and smile knowing that we tried our very best.

The Last Lecture's Living Legacy

Of all the legacies I've encountered, Professor Randy Pausch's remains my favorite.

Pausch was a computer science professor at Carnegie Mellon University. When he was just forty-six years old, terminal cancer attacked his pancreas. With only a few months left to live, he poured his remaining energy into one last stunning lecture on fulfilling childhood dreams and grasping life with gusto.

Despite his grim diagnosis, Pausch brimmed with humor, wisdom, and inspirational positivity. When his talk was posted online, its sincerity about finding purpose and pursuing one's dreams touched millions. Not one to sulk and feel sorry for himself, he persevered for another vibrant year, spinning his lecture into a bestselling book and multiple television interviews.

Pausch's greatest motivation was leaving a loving legacy to his three young children, whom he would never get to see grow up. He movingly envisioned his lecture as a message in a bottle—something they could revisit long after he was gone to feel his presence.

Through his passionate lecture, Pausch created an enduring global message to seize joy and persevere despite huge obstacles. It still changes lives today. I urge you to take a moment to witness Randy's uplifting lecture for yourself at Carnegie Mellon's website.* Let the warmth of his enduring spirit rekindle your own

---

* Watch "The Last Lecture" at cmu.edu/randyslecture.

dreams. It may even inspire you to create a video for your own loved ones.

How Will You Be Remembered?

What do you hope people will remember about you long after you're gone? Most folks want their legacy to reflect their positive attributes—ideals, values, accomplishments—not how much money they had. Once you envision what you want your legacy to look like, formulate it into a milestone to ensure it comes to fruition.

Here are some common themes to help get your creative juices flowing:

Generosity: People can remember the good you did for others, such as donating cash to causes, funding scholarships, chipping in to build hospitals, or the hours you spent volunteering at a center for disabled individuals.

Achievement: Your accomplishments in business, politics, the arts, school, sports, or any other area in which you shine can leave a lasting impression.

Innovation/Discovery: Perhaps you will leave a mark by pioneering ingenious new ways for people to think, work, or do things.

Compassion: Or maybe you'll be someone people remember for always having lent a hand or an ear to those who needed it most.

A life that had purpose and made contributions that will resonate doesn't just generate warm and fuzzy feelings for yourself—it will make your descendants proud too.

Carrying on a Legacy Can Be as Simple as Being You

In the film *Inception*, protagonist Dom Cobb and his team set out to implant a profound idea in the mind of Robert Fischer, the son of billionaire energy tycoon Maurice Fischer, at the behest of one of Fischer's corporate rivals, a man named Saito.

Maurice built the giant Fischer Morrow conglomerate that threatens to monopolize the industry. Saito, seeking to take advantage of Maurice's failing health and dissolve this emerging juggernaut, hires Cobb to strategically perform an inception on Robert. The concept of inception in the movie involves using dream-sharing technology to infiltrate the subconscious mind of a target and then implant an idea that will spur the target to act a certain way. In simpler terms, it's a way to manipulate someone, without their knowledge, to do something for your own gain. Saito's goal is to trigger Robert Fischer to dismantle his father's empire from within for the benefit of Saito's company.

In a meticulously constructed, snow-laden mountain dreamscape, Cobb skillfully guides Robert to unlock a pivotal vault—a metaphorical chamber containing his ailing father and his innermost thoughts and emotional family history instead of the military or corporate secrets filmgoers may have expected.

As Robert walks into the vault, he hears his father mutter, "Dis . . . I was dis . . . dis . . ." When Robert replies, "I know, Dad. I know you were disappointed I couldn't be you."

Then his father mutters, "No . . . no, no . . . I was disappointed that you *tried* . . ." And then Maurice raises his shaky right hand and points to a safe under his bedside table. Robert looks over, afraid of what he might find, and hesitantly punches in the code 528491.

Inside, on the top shelf, lies Maurice's last will and testament.

But more importantly, underneath, Robert finds a childhood toy, a homemade pinwheel he played with as a boy that we see him holding in an old photo framed on his dying father's bedside table.

As Robert processes the torrent of relief, longing, responsibility, and love represented by this toy, he realizes his father's pride and high standards sprang from deep affection, not rejection, as he had long believed. Robert is finally ready to chart a new course for Fischer Morrow, just as his father (but really Saito) wished.*

When it comes to keeping up a family legacy, the pressure can be great. However, it may be enough just to be your own person and chart your own course.

A Family Legacy Means Protecting Them

You need to put safeguards in place if you want to enable your children to follow their own paths. Protecting your family's legacy and ensuring the well-being of your children after you're gone involves thoughtful financial planning, legal considerations, and a comprehensive estate plan.

Here are some key estate planning milestones you can target to protect your family and your legacy:

> **Create a will:** A will is a legal document that outlines how your assets will be distributed after your death. It allows you to specify who will inherit your property, including financial accounts, real estate, and personal belongings.

> **Establish a trust:** The next step up from a will is a revocable living trust. A trust can provide more control over the distribution of assets and is particularly useful if you have substantial assets or specific wishes regarding how and when your children will receive their inheritance. Trusts

---

* *Inception* scene: youtube.com/watch?v=vlyBuG4j_8k

can also offer tax benefits and will keep your estate out of the hands of an expensive probate court.

Name legal guardians: If your children are minors, it's crucial to designate legal guardians for them in your will. This ensures that there's a plan in place for their care and upbringing in case both you and your spouse pass away. Make a list of people you trust the most and ask them if they are willing to be your children's legal guardians if you pass.

Purchase life insurance: Life insurance can provide financial security for your family in the event of your death. The payout can cover living expenses, education costs, and other financial obligations. The best time to get life insurance is around age thirty. That's when life tends to get more complicated with children and housing debt, but you're still young and healthy enough to keep your premiums low. The best type of life insurance to get at age thirty is a thirty-year term life policy.

Educate and instill values in your children: Beyond financial matters, consider imparting important values you wish your children to carry on. Arm them with the knowledge to make optimal decisions. Tell your children stories that can be passed down for generations. From educating them about money to passing down family traditions, your help and insights will benefit them and also protect your legacy.

Document important information: Create a death file that includes important information about your assets, financial accounts, insurance policies, usernames and passwords, and instructions for where to find certain things. Share this document with a trusted family member or advisor and update it as needed.

Communicate openly: Talk openly with your family about your wishes, including the details of your estate plan and any specific arrangements you've made. This can help avoid confusion and disputes in the future. You can also record yourself giving instructions and save the file with your estate documents for further clarity.

Consult with professionals: Seek guidance from financial advisors, estate planning attorneys, and tax professionals who can provide valuable insights and help tailor your plan to your family's specific needs.

Your exact approach for your estate plan will depend on your individual circumstances, which includes your financial situation, and family dynamics. It's always a good idea to consult with professionals to ensure your estate plan aligns with your goals and adequately protects your family's legacy. Please see the Further Reading section for links to *Financial Samurai* posts that delve deeper into the above suggestions.

A Conversation with an Estate Planning Lawyer

When our children arrived, my wife and I set up revocable living trusts, with the help of an estate attorney, to ensure that our kids and assets will be taken care of if either of us die prematurely. When we first met with the attorney, she insightfully noted, "People who aren't rich might need estate planning more than rich people, because they might not be able to afford to pay probate fees in the case of an untimely death."

Leave it to America's convoluted legal system to make it cumbersome and expensive to pass down assets after you die. Without a will or trust, heirs typically pay 3 to 8 percent of an estate's gross value in various probate fees, a process that can potentially drag on for more than a year. These expenses include everything from court fees to legal and accounting bills, appraisals, bond premiums, and other miscellaneous costs.

In contrast, settling a revocable trust averages only 1 to 3 percent in total fees. Yet, for me, privacy is the greater benefit. As a stealth wealth practitioner, I don't want a public reckoning of my holdings and distributions. With clear directives and lower taxes, a revocable trust makes passing down assets easier.

Estate Planning Advice to Keep in Mind

Once you have children, proper estate planning is a must. It takes effort to get your documents in order, but the benefits are well worth it.

Here are three pieces of estate-related advice based on insights I gleaned from my estate planning lawyer.

1) Reckon with your mortality

Of all assets, time remains the most precious and finite. Estate planning makes us confront this truth, but for good reason.

In my twenties and thirties, surviving to the age of sixty felt sufficient. I left full-time work at thirty-four partly to minimize regret. Fatherhood shifted my outlook. Now, I hope to make it at least to age seventy-five so I can witness our children blossom into well-adjusted, independent adults. I will die happy if I get to see them thrive in adulthood. Then, I'll lament not having had children sooner.

2) Project your wealth—and future estate tax scenarios

A significant downside of not practicing effective consumption smoothing and dying with too much is the tax burden placed upon your heirs. It's important not to overlook the power of compounding, as doing so can lead to grossly miscalculating how much wealth you are likely to accumulate in your remaining years.

Although the estate tax exemption thresholds are quite high as I write this, thanks to the Tax Cuts and Jobs Act of 2017, they are set to expire on January 1, 2026, unless Congress passes an extension.

Here's an example of just how much the estate tax exemption amount in the year of your death can affect what your heirs owe. Let's say the estate tax exemption amount for individuals is $13.61 million with a 40 percent tax rate. If you die unmarried under those terms with an impressive $23.61 million, the estate taxes due would be 40 percent of the $10 million difference between your estate and the exemption amount, or $4 million. But get this: If you die in a year when the estate tax exemption is $5 million with a 50 percent tax rate, your heirs will owe $9.3 million, more than twice as much!

I hope this extreme example helps you visualize the impact taxes can have and further appreciate the benefits of spending down your fortune before you go.

3) Give and enjoy more wealth while living, not after you're dead

Unless your children are independently wealthy, they may need help with adulting. Instead of leaving them your fortune after you're gone, it may be better to help them buy that home or pay for your grandchildren's expensive college tuition while you're still alive. That way, you'll get to help your children when they need it the most and enjoy the benefits of your giving as well.

In my opinion, it's better to spend on yourself, your loved ones, and the causes you care about when you're alive than to relinquish additional millions posthumously via taxes. So, if you expect you'll accumulate more than the estate tax exemption, get busy decumulating now.

Make Sure You Matter

Opportunities are more fleeting than you realize. Don't dwell on vague promises of *someday*. The time is now. When your life concludes, you'll want it to have mattered.

In contemplating our own mortality, we recognize our chance to leave a lasting legacy that transcends the constraints of time. Legacy is more than just a record of our life's deeds. It represents a dynamic narrative of our very essence.

Live with intention. Embrace values that resonate with your soul and leave a legacy that inspires generations to come. May your influence endure. Life is often strewn with regrets upon reflection, but you can dull their sting by paying it forward in the afterlife.

THE *FINANCIAL SAMURAI* WAY

To Contemplate:

☐ Take a moment to reflect on what you want to be remembered for. Think about how you matter today and what legacy you want to leave in the future.

☐ Toss out the conventional thinking that estate planning is only for the superrich. Revocable living trusts can be even more important for those with modest means due to the substantial costs associated with probate.

To Do:

☐ Watch Randy Pausch's "The Last Lecture" in full at cmu .edu/randyslecture.

☐ Formulate specific milestones for your ideal legacy and take proactive steps to shape that narrative through your actions today.

- ☐ Safeguard your legacy and ensure the well-being of your family with a comprehensive estate plan.

- ☐ Outline a clear succession of your assets to reinforce the effect you've had on your family's future.

- ☐ Estimate your projected net worth at death and anticipate potential changes in estate tax thresholds and rates. This forward-thinking approach will allow you to make informed decisions about your wealth and how it will be distributed.

- ☐ Watch *Inception*'s vault scene to understand the importance of being your own person.

- ☐ Aim to leave this world knowing that you mattered. Take actions that shape your legacy and ensure that the impact you've made endures beyond your lifetime.

Time to Focus and Take Action

YOUR MILESTONE JOURNEY TO BECOMING a millionaire will be full of starts and stops. But, as my favorite Chinese proverb goes, if the direction is correct, sooner or later, you will get there. I hope this book has helped steer you in the right direction. Remember, it's not enough just to read about how to become a millionaire. You must also take action based on the recommendations I've made in this book.

One of the best guiding principles is to think in probabilities instead of absolutes. As I suggest in my *Wall Street Journal* bestseller, *Buy This, Not That*, if you believe there's a 70 percent probability you're making the right decision, go for it, with the humility to understand that 30 percent of the time you're going to get it wrong. Unless your mistake is fatal, you're going to learn from it and come back stronger.

Some say that once you've won the game, you should stop playing. I say, keep on playing—staying intentional pays off in the long run. Just be careful about taking excess risk. Remember, you're not just trying to build wealth for your own well-being. You're also looking to build wealth for your family. Providing a life better than the one you grew up with is at the heart of all human striving.

Whenever you are in doubt about your investments or your efforts, extend the time frame. Watching your stocks and real estate holdings take a 20 percent dive just a year after you bought them will hurt, no doubt. However, if you zoom out and extend the time frame to ten, fifteen, or twenty years, you'll see that things usually work out.

The First Rule of Financial Independence

No matter the amount of wealth you aim to accumulate to fulfill your needs and aspirations, remember the cardinal rule of financial independence: avoid financial disasters. Once you've reached a comfortable, seven-figure net worth capable of sustaining your family indefinitely, it's wise to reduce your exposure to risk.

At the most cautious end of the spectrum, once you have sufficient funds, you could opt to invest your entire net worth in thirty-year Treasury bonds, ensuring protection against losses. However, you may be tempted to embrace greater risks once you've built a financial safety net. Just exercise caution to avoid accumulating debt or overextending yourself after winning the game of money. A significant financial setback could result in the waste of precious time in attempts to recover the losses.

Compete on Time and Freedom

Through New York and San Francisco acquaintances, I've socialized with dozens of centimillionaires and a few billionaires over the years. Contrary to popular assumptions, their levels of joy and fulfillment rarely eclipse those of the average millionaire next door.

For example, a tech founder I met who is worth $100 million

fixates on his peers who became multibillionaires. By comparing upward, he feels like a failure, despite his own nine-figure fortune. Meanwhile, an executive at a public company admits hating her job's role of battling activists and media scrutiny. Rather than enjoying her time skiing in Aspen with family, she grinds through the holidays in New York City, oppressed by work and the scrutiny involved in having thousands of shareholders and employees.

Ironically, I doubt any of these ultra-wealthy folks would be willing to give up their vast fortunes to be less stressed and happier. Just know that being a millionaire or multimillionaire won't solve all your problems. Rather, being rich might amplify your other problems, since you won't have to worry as much about paying your bills.

By all means, diligently build your million-dollar bounty through your career, investing, and entrepreneurship. But don't assume you'll discover nirvana upon arrival. For some, the next summit always beckons.

If you insist on competing with your peers, avoid using bank balances as the scoreboard once you have enough. Instead, compete for who has the most amount of *time and freedom*. I'd wager that pensioner with a paid-off house and enough savings is richer at heart than the harried millionaire still chasing their next big deal. No rational forty-year-old would trade places with a ninety-year-old billionaire. You can always make another dollar, but you can never make another minute of time.

Going Beyond the Millionaire Milestones

To all those striving toward millionaire status, I wish you fortitude and faith. Stay encouraged by the knowledge that the path delineated by my milestones leads toward open vistas full of possibility. The journey itself often proves most rewarding, an insight you may only fully grasp when looking back.

When you do finally join the millionaire circle, pause to reflect. Each zero in your net worth represents years of discipline, growth, and perseverance through uncertainty. Also realize that some luck and privilege likely assisted you—a supportive family, an influential mentor, or a friend who gifted you this book. We all stand on others' shoulders. Pay that gift forward.

After your basic needs are met, you gain the freedom to pursue higher goals that align with your personal values—rewarding work, deeper connections, and leaving an honorable legacy. Financial independence enables you to shift your focus beyond material constraints to what matters most. Yet, true contentment still springs from within. Don't endlessly compare yourself to wealthier peers; someone will always be wealthier than you. Instead, appreciate the things you already have.

Congratulations on making it this far! I'm so excited for what's in store for you. We've covered quite a lot in this book, and I hope you'll reference it frequently throughout your journey. Don't forget to celebrate as you check off each task at the end of each chapter. And keep these four themes at the core of your path forward:

1. Adopt a prosperous mindset.

2. Get on the right side of growth.

3. Live a life true to your values.

4. Leave a meaningful legacy.

Thank you for taking part in the *Millionaire Milestones* journey. If you ever need assistance or have questions, feel free to visit financialsamurai.com and drop a comment on any of the 2,500-plus articles I've written since 2009. And sign up for my free weekly newsletter at financialsamurai.com/news. Your messages are always welcome, and I'll be there to help.

Acknowledgments

Thanks to Noah Schwartzberg, my editor, for helping make this second book with Portfolio possible. It's been so pleasant working with you again. Thanks also to Leila Sandlin, assistant editor, for your helpful feedback and ideas, and to the production team for your thorough and vital copyedits and formatting.

A big thank-you to Sydney, my incredible wife, for your late nights and long hours over the course of many, many months. Your research, editorial work, input, and organization helped polish this book into what it is today. Thanks for all the heavy lifting!

To my dear kids, you are my heart and joy, forever and always. Thank you for all of your smiles and laughter throughout the journey to get this book published. I can't wait to take you on treasure hunts to find it in bookstores. Your uninhibited happiness and excitement are what keep me going. Hugs to booboo and sweetie pie.

Thank you, Colleen Kong-Savage, for your beautiful illustrations. It was a pleasure working with you again and being able to feature your artistic talents. Thank you, Rebekah Curry, for more than twenty-five years of amazing insights, love, and support. Thank you, Justy Kong, for your boundless exuberance. And thank you, Keiah Kong, for keeping me motivated throughout this project.

To the *Financial Samurai* readers, thank you for your continued support and for sharing your perspectives every time I publish a new post, newsletter, or podcast.

Finally, I would like to acknowledge the support and love of my family. I feel so blessed to have you in my life every single day.

Further Reading

IF YOU FOUND THIS BOOK valuable, please share it with your family, friends, and colleagues. Everybody deserves to achieve greater wealth and financial independence sooner rather than later.

Sign up for the free *Financial Samurai Newsletter* at financial samurai.com/news so you never miss a thing. Its features include stock market insights, real estate strategies, career and business advice, early retirement guidance, entrepreneurship tips, and special promotions.

You can also subscribe to *The Financial Samurai Podcast* on Apple (financialsamurai.com/apple) or Spotify (financialsamurai .com/spotify). On the podcast, I interview investors, authors, entrepreneurs, educators, freelancers, and other interesting guests who can help you live a better life.

For a deeper dive into some key topics covered in this book, as well as related topics, see the following posts on *Financial Samurai* and the other resources included below:

GETTING STARTED
Perspective—Seize the Millionaire Mindset

MILESTONE 1 | Find Your Why

Regret Minimization: "Conduct a Regret Minimization Exercise to Help You Move Forward," financialsamurai.com/regret-minimization-framework-exercise.

Why $1 Million Is Now $3 Million: "Are You a Real Millionaire? $3 Million Is the New $1 Million," financialsamurai.com/are-you-a-real-millionaire-3-million-new-1-million.

Retiring on $5 Million: "Is Five Million Dollars Enough to Retire Comfortably or Early?," financialsamurai.com/is-five-million-dollars-enough-to-retire-comfortably-or-early.

Health Benefits of Early Retirement: "The Health Benefits of Early Retirement Are Priceless," financialsamurai.com/the-health-benefits-of-early-retirement-are-priceless.

Golden Handcuffs: "Overcoming the Downer of No Longer Making Maximum Money," financialsamurai.com/making-maximum-money.

MILESTONE 2 | Believe You Can Be a Millionaire Too

Mistakes to Avoid at Work: "A List of Career-Limiting Moves to Blow Up Your Future," financialsamurai.com/a-list-of-career-limiting-moves-to-blow-up-your-life.

Six-Figure Salaries: "How to Make Six Figures a Year at Almost Any Age," financialsamurai.com/how-to-make-six-figures-income-at-almost-any-age.

Wall Street Jobs: "Should I Work on Wall Street? The Pros of Working in Finance," financialsamurai.com/should-i-work-on -wall-street.

Savings Targets by Age: "How Much Savings Should I Have Accumulated by Age?," financialsamurai.com/how-much-savings -should-i-have-accumulated-by-age.

One Percent Net Worth by Age: "The Top One Percent Net Worth Levels by Age Group," financialsamurai.com/the-top-one -percent-net-worth-levels-by-age-group.

Top Ways to Make Passive Income: "Ranking the Best Passive Income Investments," financialsamurai.com/ranking-the -best-passive-income-investments.

PHASE I
Growth—Millionaire Fundamentals

MILESTONE 3 | Harness the Power of Momentum

Improve Your 401(k): "How to Better Manage Your 401(k) for Retirement Success," financialsamurai.com/how-to-better -manage-your-401k-for-retirement-through-scenario-analysis.

Social Security Tips: "Social Security Strategies for a Better Retirement," financialsamurai.com/social-security-strategies-for-a -better-retirement.

What Is FIRE?: "The Fundamentals of FIRE (Financial Independence Retire Early)," financialsamurai.com/the -fundamentals-of-fire-financial-independence-retire-early.

Coast FIRE: "What Is Coast FIRE and Is It the Right Retirement Path for You?," financialsamurai.com/what-is-coast-fire-financial -independence-retire-early.

Early Retirement Amounts: "After-Tax Investment Amounts by Age to Comfortably Retire Early," financialsamurai.com/after-tax -investment-amounts-by-age-to-retire-early.

What Is Rule 72(t)?: "Use Rule 72(t) to Withdraw Money Penalty Free from an IRA," financialsamurai.com/rule-72t-to-withdraw -money-penalty-free-from-ira-for-early-retirement.

Cons of Retiring Early: "The Dark Side of Early Retirement: The Downsides of Not Working," financialsamurai.com/the-dark-side -of-early-retirement-risks-dangers.

MILESTONE 4 | Embrace the Joy of Saving and Investing

How to Invest: "DIY Investing: An Easy Guide to Investing Your Own Money," financialsamurai.com/diy-investing.

Fear-Based Saving: "Perpetual Failure: The Reason Why I Continue to Save So Much," financialsamurai.com/perpetual -failure-the-reason-why-i-continue-to-save-so-much.

Disciplined Saving: "Long Term Investing Is All About Saving Yourself from Yourself," financialsamurai.com/long-term -investing-is-all-about-saving-yourself-from-yourself.

How Much Americans Save: "Personal Saving Rate," fred .stlouisfed.org/series/PSAVERT.

Saving Rate by Country: "Saving Rate," data.oecd.org/natincome /saving-rate.htm.

MILESTONE 5 | Build Net Worth for Security and Cash Flow for Life

Net Worth by Age: "Suggested Net Worth Growth Target Rates by Age," financialsamurai.com/suggested-net-worth-growth -targets-by-age.

Cash Flow: "Always Work on Improving Cash Flow for Financial Independence," financialsamurai.com/improve-cash-flow-for -financial-independence.

Stress-Free Cash Flow: "Cash Management Is Really All About Stress Management," financialsamurai.com/building-savings-war -chest-is-about-stress-management.

Investment-Expense Mentality: "Treat All Investments as Expenses If You Want to Grow Richer," financialsamurai.com /get-richer-treat-investments-as-expenses.

How Much Americans Spend: "Average Consumer Expenditure per Year Proves Americans Are Living the Dream," financial samurai.com/the-average-consumer-expenditure-in-america.

MILESTONE 6 | Accelerate Your Wealth with Real Estate

Property-Inspection Tips: "10 Warning Signs Before Buying a House: Be a Thorough Inspector," financialsamurai.com /warning-signs-to-look-out-for-before-buying-a-house.

Choosing a Broker: "How Bad Real Estate Agents Can Cost Sellers a Lot of Money," financialsamurai.com/bad-real-estate -agents.

Dual Agency: "What Is Dual Agency? And Why Some Real Estate Agents Hate It," financialsamurai.com/dual-agency-and -why-some-real-estate-agents-hate-it.

Real Estate Commissions: "The NAR Settlement's Impact on Commissions and Home Prices," financialsamurai.com/nar -settlement-impact-real-estate-commissions-home-prices.

Safeguard Your Down Payment: "How to Invest Your Down Payment If You're Planning to Buy a House," financialsamurai.com /how-to-invest-your-down-payment-if-youre-planning-to-buy-a-house.

Selling Bonds to Buy Property: "Real Estate Is Like a Bond Plus Investment: More Potential Upside," financialsamurai.com/real -estate-is-like-a-bond-plus-investment.

Unexpected Expenses of Homeownership: "All the Surprising Costs That Come After a Home Purchase," financialsamurai .com/all-the-surprising-costs-that-come-after-a-home-purchase.

Investing in Real Estate Crowdfunding: "Private Real Estate Learning Center," financialsamurai.com/real-estate-crowd funding-learning-center.

Home-to-Car Ratio: "The Right House-to-Car Ratio for Financial Freedom," financialsamurai.com/house-to-car-ratio-for -financial-freedom.

How Much to Spend on a Car: "The 1/10th Rule for Car Buying Everyone Must Follow," financialsamurai.com/the-110th-rule-for -car-buying-everyone-must-follow.

MILESTONE 7 | Win Big with Entrepreneurship

Importance of an Online Presence: "Why You Need to Start Your Own Website Today," financialsamurai.com/why-you-need -to-start-your-own-website-today.

When to Take a Leap: "How Much Do I Have to Make as an Entrepreneur to Replace My Day Job Income?," financialsamurai

.com/how-much-do-i-have-to-make-as-an-entrepreneur-or
-contractor-to-replace-my-day-job-income.

Better Branding. "How to Build a Stronger Brand for Your Business, Blog, or Career," financialsamurai.com/how-to-build-a-stronger-brand-for-your-business-blog-and-career.

Online Entrepreneurship: "The 10 Best Reasons to Start an Online Business," financialsamurai.com/the-best-10-reasons-to-start-an-online-business.

Lifestyle Perks: "Why Start a Business? A Better Life of Course," financialsamurai.com/why-start-a-business-work-retreats-better-life.

Don't Give Up: "The Secret to Your Success: 10 Years of Unwavering Commitment," financialsamurai.com/the-secret-to-your-success-10-years-of-unwavering-commitment.

PHASE II
Lifestyle—The Millionaire Way of Life

MILESTONE 8 | Evade Financial Land Mines and Conquer the Unexpected

Inability to Outperform: "Active Versus Passive Investing Performance in Stocks and Bonds," financialsamurai.com/active-versus-passive-investing-performance-equities-fixed-income.

Higher Credit Score: "How to Improve Your Credit Score to 800 and Higher," financialsamurai.com/how-to-improve-your-credit-score-to-over-800.

Debt Grades: "Ranking Debt Types from Worst to Best," financialsamurai.com/ranking-debt-types.

Dangers of Greed: "Inflation and Greed: The Biggest Wealth Destroyers for Families," financialsamurai.com/inflation-and -greed-the-biggest-wealth-destroyers-for-families.

Margin Trading: "Losing All Your Money Investing on Margin Is Not the Worst Thing," financialsamurai.com/losing-all-your -money-investing-on-margin-is-not-the-worst-thing.

Day Trading: "Day Trading Is a Waste of Time and Money, Don't Do It!," financialsamurai.com/day-trading-is-a-waste-of-time-and -money.

Investment Risk: "The Main Types of Investment Risk Exposure to Be Aware Of," financialsamurai.com/main-types-risk-exposure -investing-hard-earned-money.

SEER Rule: "Financial SEER: A Way to Quantify Risk Tolerance and Determine Appropriate Equity Exposure," financialsamurai .com/seer-quantify-risk-tolerance-determine-appropriate-equity -exposure.

Bankruptcy: "Debt and Bankruptcy Go Together Like a Horse and Carriage," financialsamurai.com/debt-and-bankruptcy-go -together-like-a-horse-and-carriage.

How to Engineer Your Layoff Ebook: "Negotiate a Severance," financialsamurai.com/how-to-make-money-quitting-your-job-2.

MILESTONE 9 | Be Where the Money Is

Perks of Pricey Metropolitan Areas: "Living in an Expensive City Can Make You Richer, Happier, and More Diplomatic," financialsamurai.com/living-in-an-expensive-city-can-make-you -richer-and-happier.

Raising a City Family: "How Much Does a Family Need to Make to Live in an Expensive City?," financialsamurai.com/how-much -does-a-family-need-to-make-to-live-in-an-expensive-city.

City Fun Outweighs Costs: "The Excitement of Living in a Big City Is Worth the Cost," financialsamurai.com/excitement-of -living-in-a-big-city-is-worth-the-cost.

How to Geoarbitrage: "The Proper Geoarbitrage Strategy: First Your City, Then Your Country, Then the World," financialsamurai.com/the-proper-geoarbitrage-strategy.

What Are Eighteen-Hour Cities?: "18-Hour Cities: An Attractive Real Estate Investment Opportunity," financialsamurai.com /18-hour-cities.

Job Mistakes to Avoid: "A List of Career-Limiting Moves to Blow Up Your Future," financialsamurai.com/a-list-of-career-limiting -moves-to-blow-up-your-life.

MILESTONE 10 | Make the Most of Your Marriage and Family

Separate Bank Accounts: "Financial Dependence Is the Worst: Why Each Spouse Needs Their Own Bank Account," financialsamurai.com/financial-dependence-is-the-worst-why -each-spouse-needs-their-own-bank-account.

Shared Financial Goals: "How Couples Can Adopt the Same Financial Goals and Win," financialsamurai.com/couples-adopt -same-financial-goals.

Wedding Costs: "Wedding Spending Rules to Follow If You Don't Want to End Up Broke and Alone," financialsamurai.com /wedding-spending-rules-to-follow-if-you-dont-want-to-end-up -broke-and-alone.

SLAT: "A Spousal Lifetime Access Trust (SLAT) for Estate Planning," financialsamurai.com/spousal-lifetime-access -trust-slat.

Financial Literacy: "Is Personal Finance in Schools Required? Money Matters!," financialsamurai.com/personal-finance-in-schools.

529 College Savings Plans: "Everything to Know About the 529 College Savings Plan," financialsamurai.com/529-college-savings -plan.

Roth IRAs: "Opening a Roth IRA for Your Kids to Build Wealth and Save on Taxes," financialsamurai.com/opening-a-roth-ira-for -your-kids.

Provider's Clock: "A Provider's Clock for Men Is Like a Biological Clock for Women," financialsamurai.com/a-providers-clock-for -men-and-a-biological-clock-for-women.

Aging Parents: "Are Your Parents Putting Your Retirement At Risk?," financialsamurai.com/parents-putting-retirement -risk.

Long-Term Care Insurance: "Should I Get Long-Term Care Insurance?," financialsamurai.com/should-i-get-long-term-care -insurance.

PHASE III
Legacy—The Millionaire's Everlasting Imprint

MILESTONE 11 | Spend Your Wealth Judiciously

Decumulation: "The Best Decumulation Age to Start Spending Down Your Fortune," financialsamurai.com/the-best-decumul ation-age.

FSWR vs. the 4 Percent Rule: "The Proper Safe Withdrawal Rate: 4 Percent Rule Is Outdated," financialsamurai.com/proper-safe-withdrawal-rate.

Preserving Principal: "The Ideal Withdrawal Rate for Retirement Does Not Touch Principal," financialsamurai.com/the-ideal-withdrawal-rate-for-retirement-doesnt-touch-principal.

Retirement Philosophies: "Two Retirement Philosophies Will Determine Your Safe Withdrawal Rate," financialsamurai.com/two-retirement-philosophies-will-determine-your-safe-withdrawal-rate.

Life Expectancy: "Your Life Expectancy Depends Greatly on Wealth and Location," financialsamurai.com/life-expectancy-depends-on-wealth-location-social-influence.

Importance of Companionship: "The Key to Living Longer: Fear Being Alone Far More Than Going Broke," financialsamurai.com/the-key-to-living-longer-and-happier.

MILESTONE 12 | Create an Immortal Legacy

Estate Planning 101: "Estate Planning Basics: Get Started Today," financialsamurai.com/estate-planning-basics.

Important Terminology: "Estate Planning Terminology You Should Know," financialsamurai.com/estate-planning-terminology.

Publish Your Memoirs: "How to Start a Blog: Insights into Building Your Own Website," financialsamurai.com/how-to-start-a-profitable-blog.

Wills and Trusts: "Will vs Trust: Which Is Better," financialsamurai.com/will-vs-trust.

Types of Life Insurance: "Different Types of Life Insurance Explained," financialsamurai.com/different-types-of-life -insurance-explained.

Purchase Life Insurance: "How to Buy Life Insurance in 7 Steps Stress-Free," financialsamurai.com/how-to-buy-life-insurance.

Estate Taxes: "Historical Estate Tax Exemption Amounts and Tax Rates," financialsamurai.com/historical-estate-tax-exemption -amounts-and-tax-rates.

What Is a Death File: "The Death File and Why You Need One," financialsamurai.com/death-file.

Randy Pausch: "The Last Lecture," cmu.edu/randyslecture.

Inception Vault Scene: youtube.com/watch?v=vlyBuG4j_8k.

Inheritance for Your Kids: "The Right Amount of Money to Give and Leave Our Children," financialsamurai.com/the-right -amount-of-money-to-give-and-leave-our-children.

Notes

Milestone 1 | Find Your Why

8 **Earning a million dollars a year:** Sam Dogen, "Who Makes a Million Dollars a Year? Exploring the Top 0.1% Income Earners," *Financial Samurai*, February 14, 2024, financialsamurai.com/who-makes-a-million-dollars-a-year-exploring-the-top-0-1-income-earners.

9 **by the time children turn nineteen:** Committee on Family Caregiving for Older Adults; Board on Health Care Services; Health and Medicine Division; National Academies of Sciences, Engineering, and Medicine; Richard Schulz and Jill Eden, eds., *Families Caring for an Aging America* (Washington, DC: National Academies Press, 2016), ncbi.nlm.nih.gov/books/NBK396403.

10 **cost to raise a child:** Rina Torchinsky, "It Now Costs $300,000 to Raise a Child," *The Wall Street Journal*, August 19, 2022, wsj.com/articles/it-now-costs-300-000-to-raise-a-child-11660864334.

10 **Cost of two years at community:** Emma Kerr and Sarah Wood, "See the Average College Tuition in 2023–2024," *US News & World Report*, September 20, 2023, usnews.com/education/best-colleges/paying-for-college/articles/paying-for-college-infographic; Melanie Hanson, "Average Cost of College & Tuition," EducationData.org, November 18, 2023, educationdata.org/average-cost-of-college.

10 **The expected all-in cost of four:** Kerr and Wood, "See the Average College Tuition in 2023–2024"; Hanson, "Average Cost of College & Tuition."

10 **Average health-care expenses:** Fidelity Viewpoints, "How to Plan for Rising Health Care Costs," fidelity.com/viewpoints/personal-finance/plan-for-rising-health-care-costs.

10 **Average annual housing and transportation:** Andrew Shilling, "This is the No. 1 Expense, by Far, for Retirement-Age Americans—and Pros Say It Shouldn't Be," *MarketWatch*, December 3, 2022, marketwatch.com/picks/is-your-retirement-spending-normal-heres-exactly-how-much-the-average-retired-household-spends-each-year-on-everything-from-housing-to-clothing-01669923485.

10 **Average annual cost of a private:** "Cost of Care Survey," Genworth.com, February 22, 2024, genworth.com/aging-and-you/finances/cost-of-care.html.

11 **For more perspective, in 2010:** Daniel Kahneman and Angus Deaton, "High Income Improves Evaluation of Life but Not Emotional Well-Being," *Proceedings of the National Academy of Sciences of the United States of America* 107, no. 38 (September 7, 2010): 16489–93, pnas.org/doi/10.1073/pnas.1011492107.

11 **In 2023, Kahneman published:** Adela Suliman, "Can Money Buy Happiness? Scientists Say It Can," *The Washington Post*, March 8, 2023, washingtonpost.com/business/2023/03/08/money-wealth-happiness-study; Aimee Picchi, "One Study Said Happiness Peaked at $75,000 in Income. Now, Economists Say It's Higher—by a Lot," CBS News, March 10, 2023, cbsnews.com/news/money-happiness-study-daniel-kahneman-500000-versus-75000.

12 **Studies even show:** Mark Borgschulte, Marius Guenzel, Canyao Liu, and Ulrike Malmendier, "CEO Stress, Aging, and Death," IZA—Institute of Labor Economics, August 2023, docs.iza.org/dp16366.pdf.

17 **only about 2,781 billionaires:** "World's Billionaires List," *Forbes*, accessed September 7, 2024, forbes.com/billionaires/.

17 **mansion like Jeff Bezos:** Hannah Towey and Katie Canales, "Amazon Founder Jeff Bezos Pledged to Donate the Majority of His Wealth to Charity. Here's How He Currently Spends His $122 Billion Fortune, from Giant Underground Clocks to Space

Exploration," *Business Insider*, November 16, 2022, businessinsider
.com/jeff-bezos-net-worth-life-spending-amazon
-founder-billion-wealth.

10 According to the Harvard Study: Harvard Medical School
and Massachusetts General Hospital, "Harvard Study of Adult
Development," Harvard Second Generation Study, 2015,
adultdevelopmentstudy.org; Liz Mineo, "Good Genes Are Nice, but
Joy Is Better," *The Harvard Gazette*, April 11, 2017, news.harvard
.edu/gazette/story/2017/04/over-nearly-80-years-harvard-study
-has-been-showing-how-to-live-a-healthy-and-happy-life.

Milestone 2: Believe You Can Be a Millionaire Too

21 **UBS Global Wealth Report:** "Global Wealth Report 2023,"
UBS.com, 2024, ubs.com/global/en/family-office-uhnw/reports
/global-wealth-report-2023.html.

21 **That equates to roughly 1 percent:** Anne Morse, "World
Population Estimated at 8 Billion," United States Census Bureau,
November 9, 2023, census.gov/library/stories/2023/11/world
-population-estimated-eight-billion.html.

21 **The Federal Reserve's Survey:** Board of Governors of the Federal
Reserve Board, "2022 Survey of Consumer Finances," November
21, 2023, federalreserve.gov/econres/scfindex.htm.

21 **Of course, the median household:** Board of Governors of the
Federal Reserve Board, "2022 Survey of Consumer Finances."

22 **roughly $1.1 million to belong:** "Global Wealth Report 2023,"
UBS.com.

22 **top 1 percent in America:** Dock David Treece, "Are You in the
Top 1%?," *Forbes Advisor*, June 8, 2023, forbes.com/advisor
/investing/financial-advisor/are-you-in-the-top-1-percent.

22 **By 2027, it estimates:** "Global Wealth Report 2023,"
UBS.com.

22 **Vermont gas station janitor:** Vishesh Raisinghani, "A Janitor in
Vermont Built an $8M Fortune Without Anyone Around Him
Knowing. These Are the 3 Simple Techniques That Made Ronald
Read Rich—and Can Do the Same for You Too," *Yahoo! Finance*,
August 29, 2023, finance.yahoo.com/news/janitor-vermont
-amassed-8m-fortune-140000770.html.

24 **Among middle-aged, college-educated:** "QuickFacts United
States," United States Census Bureau, accessed July 1, 2023, census

.gov/quickfacts/fact/table/US/PST045221; Victoria Stilwell, "What Are Your Odds of Becoming a Millionaire?," *Bloomberg,* January 21, 2016, bloomberg.com/features/2016-millionaire-odds.

26 **He started investing at age:** "The Warren Buffett & Berkshire Hathaway Timeline," Warren Buffett Archive, CNBC, 2018, buffett.cnbc.com/buffett-timeline.

26 **By his early thirties:** Paul Sisolak, "How Rich Warren Buffett Was at Your Age," *Business Insider,* August 12, 2015, businessinsider.com/how-rich-warren-buffett-was-at-your-age -2015-8.

26 **He reached billionaire status:** Sisolak, "How Rich Warren Buffett Was at Your Age"; "Profile: Warren Buffett," *Forbes,* accessed August 24, 2024, forbes.com/profile/warren-buffett /?sh=146f22f84639.

26 **Studies show that everybody's:** Victoria Stilwell, "What Are Your Odds of Becoming a Millionaire?"

Milestone 3: Harness the Power of Momentum

33 **the historical annual return:** Lorie Konish, "The S&P 500 Is Up About 23% Year to Date. Investors in That Index Should 'Set a Strategy and Stay Invested,' Expert Says," CNBC, December 15, 2023, cnbc.com/2023/12/15/the-sp-500-is-up-over-23percent -year-to-date-what-to-know-before-investing.html.

33 **Some investment houses:** Sam Dogen, "Finishing Rich Despite A Low-Return Stock Market Environment," *Financial Samurai,* October 23, 2024, financialsamurai.com/low-stock-market-return -scenario; Muslim Farooque, "Goldman Sachs Predicts Sluggish S&P 500 Growth Over Next Decade, Warns of Lower Returns," *Yahoo Finance,* October 21, 2024, finance.yahoo.com/news /goldman-sachs-predicts-sluggish-p-192356002.html; JP Morgan Asset Management, "2025 Long-Term Capital Market Assumptions," accessed October 23, 2024, am.jpmorgan.com/us /en/asset-management/institutional/insights/portfolio-insights /ltcma/; Vanguard Investment Strategy Group, "Market Perspectives," Vanguard, October 16, 2024, advisors.vanguard .com/insights/article/series/market-perspectives.

33 **roughly 70 percent of the time:** Keith Speights, "The S&P 500 Is Poised to Do Something It's Only Done 3 Times Ever. Here's What History Says It Could Mean for Stocks in 2024," *Yahoo!*

Finance, December 24, 2023, finance.yahoo.com/news/p-500
-poised-something-only-104900192.html.

33 **employees under fifty years old:** "401(k) Limit Increases to $23,000
for 2024, IRA Limit Rises to $7,000," IRS.gov, November 1, 2023,
irs.gov/newsroom/401k-limit-increases-to-23000-for-2024-ira
-limit-rises-to-7000.

37 **According to a survey by:** Sarah O'Brien, "62% of Workers View
401(K) Employer Match as Key to Reaching Retirement Goals.
But They May Wait Years for Those Contributions to Be Their
Own," CNBC, April 14, 2022, cnbc.com/2022/04/14/62percent
-of-workers-view-employer-401k-match-as-key-way-to-reach
-retirement.html.

43 **Your chances of earning:** Trevor Jennewine, "Here's the Average
Stock Market Return in Every Month of the Year," February 6,
2024, *The Motley Fool*, fool.com/investing/2024/02/06/average
-stock-market-return-in-every-month-of-year.

Milestone 4: Embrace the Joy of Saving and Investing

52 **According to data from the:** US Bureau of Economic Analysis,
"Personal Saving Rate (PSAVERT)," FRED, Federal Reserve Bank
of St. Louis, accessed April 26, 2024, fred.stlouisfed.org/graph
/?g=580A.

52 **With such a low saving rate:** Aditya Aladangady et al., *Changes in
US Family Finances from 2019 to 2022: Evidence from the Survey
of Consumer Finances* (Washington, DC: Board of Governors of
the Federal Reserve System, October 2023), doi.org/10.17016
/8799.

52 **In January 2020, the average:** FRED, US Bureau of Economic
Analysis, "Personal Saving Rate (PSAVERT)," accessed March 29,
2024.

52 **If you long to become:** Aladangady et al., *Changes in U.S. Family
Finances from 2019 to 2022*.

Milestone 5: Build Net Worth for Security
and Cash Flow for Life

59 **Paying any more than a:** "IRS Provides Tax Inflation Adjustment
for Tax Year 2024," IRS.gov, November 9, 2023, irs.gov
/newsroom/irs-provides-tax-inflation-adjustments-for-tax-year
-2024.

Milestone 6: Accelerate Your Wealth with Real Estate

73 **This one-two combination:** Melissa Dittmann Tracey, "Study: Homeowner Wealth Is 40 Times Higher Than Renters," *Realtor Magazine*, April 18, 2023, nar.realtor/magazine/real-estate-news/study-homeowner-wealth-is-40-times-higher-than-renters.

74 **In the past sixty years:** World Bank, "Inflation, Consumer Prices for the United States (FPCPITOTLZGUSA)," FRED, Federal Reserve Bank of St. Louis, accessed December 19, 2023, fred .stlouisfed.org/series/FPCPITOTLZGUSA.

75 **For reference, the annualized:** Sean Ross, "Has Real Estate or the Stock Market Performed Better Historically?," Investopedia, December 19, 2023, investopedia.com/ask/answers/052015/which -has-performed-better-historically-stock-market-or-real-estate.asp; "US House Price Index YoY (I: USCHPIY)," YCharts.com, accessed January 28, 2024, ycharts.com/indicators/us_house _price_index_yoy#; G. Brian Davis, "Real Estate vs. Stocks: What 145 Years of Returns Tells Us," *BiggerPockets*, March 10, 2023, biggerpockets.com/blog/real-estate-vs-stocks -performance.

77 **His compound return from 1965:** Yun Li, "Warren Buffett, Who Turns 93, Is at the Top of His Game as He Pushes Berkshire Hathaway to New Heights," CNBC, August 30, 2023, cnbc .com/2023/08/30/warren-buffett-is-at-the-top-of-his-game-as -berkshire-hits-new-heights.html.

83 **Sources: US Census Bureau:** US Census Bureau and US Department of Housing and Urban Development, "Median Sales Price of Houses Sold for the United States (MSPUS)," FRED, Federal Reserve Bank of St. Louis, accessed March 27, 2024, fred .stlouisfed.org/series/MSPUS.

84 **the typical first-time homebuyer:** Khristopher J. Brooks, "It's Taking Americans Much Longer in Life to Buy Their First Home," CBS News, August 15, 2023, cbsnews.com/news/average -homebuyer-age-millennial-data-realtor.

87 **NAR agreed to pay:** Rob Wile, "Home Buyers and Sellers to Be Spared Standard Broker Commissions Under $418 Million Settlement," NBC News, March 15, 2024, nbcnews.com /business/real-estate/national-association-realtors-approves-418 -million-settlement-rcna143577.

92   **Buying too much car:** Sam Dogen, "The Right House-to-Car Ratio for Financial Freedom," *Financial Samurai*, June 27, 2024, financialsamurai.com/house-to-car-ratio-for-financial-freedom/; US Census Bureau, "Real Median Household Income in the United States (MEHOINUSA672N)," FRED, Federal Reserve Bank of St. Louis, accessed September 12, 2023, fred.stlouisfed .org/series/MEHOINUSA672N.

Milestone 7: Win Big with Entrepreneurship

95   **Creators of massively successful companies:** Rob LaFranco, Grace Chung, and Chase Peterson-Withorn, eds., "World's Billionaires List," *Forbes*, 2024, www.forbes.com/billionaires.

98   **The average millionaire has *seven*:** Andrew Lisa, "7 Income Streams That Make Millionaires Rich," *Yahoo! Finance*, May 18, 2023, finance.yahoo.com/news/7-income-streams-millionaires -rich-200008107.html.

99   **For example, in 1978:** "The Dollar-a-Year Man," *Forbes*, May 8, 2002, updated June 6, 2013, forbes.com/2002/05/08/0508iacocca .html?sh=584e82951c34.

104   **roughly two times the median:** US Census Bureau, "Real Median Household Income in the United States (MEHOINUSA672N)," FRED, Federal Reserve Bank of St. Louis, accessed September 12, 2023, fred.stlouisfed.org/series/MEHOINUSA672N.

Milestone 8: Evade Financial Land Mines and Conquer the Unexpected

113   **For example, a retired law enforcement:** Katrin Bennhold, Clare Toeniskoetter, and Lynsea Garrison, "How One Family Lost $900,000 in a Timeshare Scam," in *The Daily*, produced by Asthaa Chaturvedi and Will Reid, podcast, April 12, 2024, nytimes.com /2024/04/12/podcasts/the-daily/scam-cartel-timeshare.html.

116   **There are even dating apps:** Chris Morris, "This New Dating App Matches Singles. But Only If They Have Good Credit Scores," *Fast Company*, February 14, 2024, fastcompany.com /91028669/new-dating-app-score-matches-singles-good-credit -scores.

124   **Studies show most employees:** Juliana Menasce Horowitz and Kim Parker, "How Americans View Their Jobs," Pew Research

Center, March 30, 2023, pewresearch.org/social-trends/2023/03
/30/how-americans-view-their-jobs.

126 **After her second worldwide concert:** Stephen Fry, "Lady Gaga
Takes Tea with Mr. Fry," *Financial Times*, May 27, 2011, ft.com
/content/0cca76f0-873a-11e0-b983-00144feabdc0.

126 **Roughly thirteen years after she:** "How Lady Gaga Built a $150
Million Fortune," *Forbes*, forbes.com/stories/billionaires
/how-lady-gaga-built-a-150-million-fortune.

Milestone 9: Be Where the Money Is

131 **Let's look at some data:** US Department of Commerce, "The
Income Ranking of Metros Has Changed Little Since 1980,"
Regional Economic Research Initiative Blog, September 6, 2023,
commerce.gov/news/blog/2023/09/income-ranking-metros-has
-changed-little-1980.

132 **Sam and Helen Walton:** Walton Family Foundation, "Our
History," waltonfamilyfoundation.org/about-us/our
-history.

132 **Meanwhile, according to Zillow:** "Little Rock, AR Housing
Market," Zillow, accessed March 31, 2024, zillow.com/home
-values/52998/little-rock-ar.

132 **Not only is Honolulu:** Mike Winters, "The 10 US Places with the
Highest Cost of Living—No. 1 Costs More Than Double the
National Average," CNBC, June 29, 2024, cnbc.com/2024/06/29
/us-highest-cost-of-living.html; Hawai'i Appleseed Center for Law
and Economic Justice, Hawai'i Budget & Policy Center, "The
High Cost of Low Wages," December 2023, hiappleseed.org
/publications/high-cost-low-wages.

134 **On average, Americans move:** "Calculating Migration
Expectancy Using ACS Data," US Census Bureau, December 3,
2021, census.gov/topics/population/migration/guidance
/calculating-migration-expectancy.html.

135 **Meanwhile, industries that primarily:** Greg Rosalsky, "Lean
Out: Employees Are Accepting Lower Pay in Order to Work
Remotely," *Planet Money*, July 12, 2022, npr.org/sections/money
/2022/07/12/1110510488/lean-out-employees-are-accepting
-lower-pay-in-order-to-work-remotely.

137 **Today, Rippling is valued:** Mehnaz Yasmin and Krystal Hu, "HR
Tech Startup Rippling Climbs to $13.5 Billion Valuation After

Coatue-Led Funding," Reuters, April 22, 2024, reuters.com
/technology/hr-tech-startup-rippling-valued-135-bln-after-latest
-fundraise-2024-04-22.

Milestone 10: Make the Most of Your
Marriage and Family

140   **While some people have started:** Eleanor Pringle, "People Have
Started Posting Their Credit Scores on Dating Profiles—It's
Winning Them More Matches and Better Dates," *Fortune*, May
31, 2023, fortune.com/2023/05/31/credit-scores-on-hinge-dating
-profiles-getting-better-matches.

140   **After all, money consistently ranks:** Barbara Greenberg, "Why
Do Couples Really Fight About Money?," *Psychology Today*, July 9,
2023, psychologytoday.com/us/blog/the-teen-doctor/202307
/why-do-couples-really-fight-about-money.

153   **Speaking of divorce, although it:** Christy Bieber, "Revealing
Divorce Statistics in 2024," *Forbes Advisor*, January 8, 2024, forbes.
com/advisor/legal/divorce/divorce-statistics.

156   **For example, the average cost:** Kerr and Wood, "See the Average
College Tuition in 2023–2024."

156   **By the year 2042 those costs:** Vanessa Wong, "In 18 Years, a College
Degree Could Cost About $500,000," *BuzzFeed News*, March 17,
2017, buzzfeednews.com/article/venessawong/in-18-years-a
-college-degree-could-cost-about-500000#.uk0Lwl171.

156   **research shows that higher education:** Zina Kumok and Alicia
Hahn, "7 Compelling Reasons Why You Should Go to College,"
Forbes Advisor, June 14, 2023, forbes.com/advisor/student-loans
/why-should-you-go-to-college.

158   **Planning for long-term care:** US Department of Health &
Human Services, "How Much Care Will You Need?,"
LongTermCare.gov, February 18, 2020, acl.gov/ltc/basic-needs
/how-much-care-will-you-need.

158   **It's incredibly expensive:** "Cost of Care Survey," accessed August
8, 2024, Genworth.com.

Milestone 11: Spend Your Wealth Judiciously

168   **The rule was formulated by:** Cooper Evan, Paul Curcio, and
David Tony, "What Is the 4% Rule?," CNN, May 17, 2024,
cnn.com/cnn-underscored/money/four-percent-rule-retirement;

CNBC, "US 10 Year Treasury," accessed September 8, 2024, cnbc .com/quotes/US10Y.

173 **dive into the blue zones:** Dan Buettner, *The Blue Zones: Lessons for Living Longer from the People Who've Lived the Longest* (Washington, DC: National Geographic Society, 2008).

173 **They counter loneliness:** Alvin Powell, "How Social Isolation, Loneliness Can Shorten Your Life," *The Harvard Gazette*, October 3, 2023, news.harvard.edu/gazette/story/2023/10 /how-social-isolation-loneliness-can-shorten-your-life; Nell Derick Debevoise, "The Power of Purpose: How Ikigai Can Help Us Live Longer," *Forbes*, October 27, 2023, forbes.com /sites/nelldebevoise/2023/10/06/the-power-of-purpose-how-ikigai -can-help-us-live-longer.

175 **Whole-body scan ($2,499):** "Pricing," Prenuvo.com, accessed February 9, 2024, prenuvo.com/pricing.

175 **These scans are primarily:** UCSF Department of Radiology & Biomedical Imaging, "Bone Density Scan (DXA or DEXA)," accessed September 8, 2024, radiology.ucsf.edu/patient -care/services/bone-density-scan-dxa-dexa.

175 **DEXA scans can also be:** UC Davis Health, "DXA Body Composition Analysis," Sports Medicine, accessed September 8, 2024, health.ucdavis.edu/sports-medicine/resources/dxa-info.

175 **Biotech company GRAIL created:** "FAQs for Patients About the Galleri Test," Galleri.com, 2024, galleri.com/patient/faqs.